Communication Essays

Also by Rodney G. Miller

Finding a Future
Australians Speak Out: Persuasive Language Styles
Communication & Beyond

Website: communicator.rodney-miller.com

Communication Essays

Rodney G. Miller

Parula Press

Communication Essays

Cover Image credit: "hand" Gerd Altmann from Pixabay

Cataloging-in-Publication Data
Name: Miller, Rodney G., author
Title: *Communication Essays*
Description: Albany, NY: Parula Press, [2022]
Rodney G. Miller; references, bibliography
Subjects: LCSH: 1. Communication – Teaching – Practice
2. Organizational Development – Leadership
3. Fundraising

ISBN: 978-1-7374895-4-2 (hardback)

Library of Congress Control Number: 2022915803

In memory of my mother and father

Table of Contents

Introduction

The seven essays selected for this book were written from 1979 to 2010. Each addresses challenges for public communication that endure still, from well before the time in which each essay was written. Strategies and processes to strengthen public discourse in a democracy or an organization's interaction with the community will always require organized personal communication.

How to develop oral communication in a multicultural society, or to counter propaganda in a democracy, or to encourage trust of an organization, or to advance an organization's relationship with its community, or to sustain funding growth for an organization through the best or worst economic times are among more substantial communication challenges.

As a digest of insights and ways to strengthen public communication, the book shares thoughts found effective to put communication understandings into practice. The ideas presented here matured in the communication classroom, at public symposia, and through three decades leading start-up or formative external relations and fundraising efforts for educational and community organizations.

Ways to jump-start higher performance communication efforts resulted from the combination of a problem-solving approach with the distillation of insights from high-performing organizations in the United States, United Kingdom, Canada, Australia, and New Zealand. Structured studies of high-performing organizations have helped to sustain ongoing learning personally. For example, informing the essays on benchmarking and funding growth are best practices distilled from conversations, interviews, and studies within more than twenty high-performing organizations.

Public communication through individual or collective effort is a stimulating and exciting force in society. I hope you will find the priorities and best practices described here helpful to encourage understanding, relationship, and action.

1: Developing Oral Communication

... to speak out - a root of democracy[1]

S.M. Halloran suggested that the *rhetor:*

> ...had interiorized all that was best in ...culture and applied this knowledge in public forums, influencing...fellow citizens to act in accord with their common cultural heritage.[2]

As teachers of communication, we are all rhetors. In a modern pluralistic society, we lack the "common cultural heritage" that it was claimed rhetors in ancient Greece enjoyed. The task of understanding our own pluralist culture is complex, but this understanding is still needed to communicate.

Lawrence Stenhouse defined culture as a complex of shared understandings that provide the medium for individuals to communicate with one another.[3] It is a commonplace to note that these shared understandings are drawn from our individual experiences of society and are consciously and unconsciously expressed in the messages of newspapers, television, radio, advertisement, and other products of the mass society. It is educational myopia to avoid teaching a self-critical awareness of culture; and anyway, language teachers cannot leave this task to others since language and culture are so closely intertwined.

I believe we must concern ourselves with more than just the acquisition of skills and the appropriateness of language use for an audience and context. Nazi speakers performed eloquent, sometimes imaginative orations,[4] appropriate to audience and context, and successfully convinced a nation that mass murder was "appropriate." The inadequacy and danger of adopting so limited a perspective on language use is widely recognized.

Dell Hymes urged that, in teaching language, the failure to deal explicitly with socio-cultural concerns is itself an ideological choice, reflecting the assumption that a person is abstract, isolated individually, almost an unmotivated cognitive mechanism.[5] Additionally, Andrew Wilkinson has commented that:

> An autocratic regime is not concerned to encourage people to talk and express themselves...[and]...the long tradition of authoritarian teaching in education has resulted in grave limitations on the oracy of the students.[6]

This observation might as readily be made about some teaching in Australia and, undoubtedly, describes what occurs in the educational systems of some other Western democracies.

Children from such schooling tend to participate in society or continue to higher education with few critical abilities. Although schools are increasingly encouraging students to develop oracy not in a narrow sense of ability to speak and listen, but to become aware of people's values,[7] the leaden weight of adult apathy to politics and social involvement remains substantial. Massive sections of the community appear to regard politics with cynicism, and many assume that the democratic process is a hollow mockery of what it is supposed to be.[8] Language teachers are rhetors who can teach children how to become more curious, more informed, and more critically involved adults.

Citizens must be politically engaged for a democracy to continue. Political oracy relates not only to the communication abilities of elected politicians but more to the ability of ordinary citizens to understand, to be involved in, and to contribute with effect to discussion that influences how government and other authorities shape parameters for living. David McLellan regrets that so much political study focuses on the way institutions work, the means of acquiring and preserving power, and the impersonal techniques of government. He sees that politics has become:

> ...a specialized profession in which only the opinions of "experts" have any weight... [and there is] ...a growing gap...between what most people experience as important to themselves and the increasingly irrelevant and mystifying manoeuvres of the public world.[9]

McLellan suggests that, because techniques are easier to deal with than values, political pundits also focus on techniques and too little develop discussion on values.[10]

How much do our students know about their own value systems? What do they understand or care about the effects of their talk with others? If our students "acquire" more effective techniques of interaction with each other, parents, and neighbors, how might they also consider the consequences of influencing others? What do our students know about the processes and ethics of communication?

In response to these and many other questions, humanities faculty at Queensland Institute of Technology seek to develop students' curiosity about their society and thereby build robust abilities in communication. Two subjects, *Australian Studies* and *Business and Society*, are especially concerned with

2

development of cultural and philosophical awareness. In *Australian Studies,* we identify repeated patterns, themes, and values in social documents such as speeches, newspaper articles, advertisements, and TV or radio programs to outline any special preoccupations of Australians. Students discuss and evaluate the nature of Australian social identity and how the expression of this identity has shaped and been shaped by the action of individuals. For example, in outlining the beginnings of the Australian Broadcasting Commission, we are interested not only in the details of the Commission's foundation but also in how it differed from or was like the British Broadcasting Commission. This tells us not only about the social context but also how part of this context is sensitive to ideas, ideologies, and mythologies from the newer culture of Australia.

This approach is enlarged upon in the later subject *Business and Society,* where students examine the philosophical concepts underlying the free enterprise system to develop an understanding of the role of business and especially the communication industry in the history and evolution of capitalism. Discussions in both subjects are critical/evaluative and stimulate students to identify practical ways of getting others to think critically and constructively about the improvement of their society. Students soon recognize that people communicating can assist one another to experience different values and value systems more fully.

Yet, while these subjects examining culture provide important groundwork, the real learning of cultural awareness and the responsibility of students to each other, to their family, and to the community occurs in practice.

For example, in a speech writing subject at QIT, students analyze different speech styles and outline the stylistic characteristics in the language of Sir Winston Churchill, Martin Luther King Jr., Krishna Menon, John Curtin, Sir Robert Menzies, or close to home, local business and political figures. Students write speeches in the styles of these people and eventually a speech for delivery by a local speaker to a community audience. This confronts students with ethical problems they will face in much communication work that is paid for in the community. Advertisers, public relations practitioners, and journalists are especially faced with ethical considerations about whether and in what way they should sell their expertise as communicators.

Only if students develop a close understanding of the values of their society and the consequences of how and what they communicate can they see their own values more clearly and act ethically to improve society. A teacher must give students a good deal of individual attention to help them develop the sophistication required to manage conflicting pressures and needs of a "client," society, and the student. A teacher must be open in this, stating personal values and encouraging informed criticism of these as much as of anyone else's stance.

Already this integrated teaching of language in its cultural context has some success.

Notable features of the program are:

1. National culture is seen as a subject worthy of study.
2. Students are introduced to additional characteristics of their community by discussing concepts and actively performing projects in the community, such as through communication internships or a project like speech writing.
3. A natural integration of cultural and communication competence is sustained.
4. Students gain in confidence, because they are guided in their entry to the application of communication abilities in the community and they become familiar with a diversity of community audiences, with whom they might later be working.
5. Students demonstrate a lively interest in developing their language ability during and after involvement in the program.

David Ingram has used similar means in foreign language teaching to achieve some similar benefits in teaching younger age groups.[11] But he recommends also the establishment of residential colleges where learners can be immersed in a foreign language for weeks or months at a time and, secondly, he recommends using activities that provide meaningful and motivating communication, such as "excursions," "French dinners," and so on.[12] A real value of such an approach is that it focuses on communication and its success, rather than on errors.[13] Students observe and assess their own performance, and the success of coming to terms with language and culture motivates these students further.

In the QIT program, we still need to extend the approach to enhance linkages to cultural observations in more subjects that are concerned with teaching communication in practical and professional areas, such as public relations and advertising especially. But the first step is made, and with "1984" almost upon us we need to seriously consider the philosophical bases of communication study and teaching.[14] It is no longer adequate to *assume* students will apply their communication abilities responsibly. They must, I believe, be encouraged to develop guidelines for deciding between potentially conflicting interests, including those of society and themselves.

Otherwise, the rationalizations of an "ocker" culture[15] may reassure our students either that all is well, or more likely encourage them to think, as Hobbes might have, that they must "rip off" others or be "ripped off," and that they must accept this as the fate of living in society. Marcus Clarke wittily showed his concern with this problem in 1877, writing that:

> [by 1977] The Australians will be freed from the highest burden of intellectual development… the average Australian will be a tall, coarse, strong-jawed,

greedy, pushing, talented man, excelling in swimming and horsemanship…
In five hundred years, unless recruited from foreign nations, the breed will
be wholly extinct; but in that five hundred years it will have changed the face
of Nature, and swallowed up all our contemporary civilization.[16]

Clarke's overstatement severely warns of the need to develop in students a
responsive awareness of the culture, the real needs and not just the "wants" of
society.

He also anticipates mass migration of other races to Australia, which of
course has since occurred, especially after the Second World War. Australia must
now consider itself to be a "pluralist society in which 21.9% of Australian born
children have at least one parent born in a non-English speaking country."[17] The
multicultural character of Australia causes special challenges in the large
population of migrants and First Nations.

This subject is so wide and complex to require address in another paper or
in discussion, but it is important to recognize that the Schools Commission:

> …regards the maintenance of home language in the school and varying
> balances between the child's first language and English primarily as a means
> of making the child and family feel at home in the school and of promoting
> English language competence.[18]

Unless Australia sustains common languages, however, it is difficult to see
how Australian society might fulfill a democratic vision. Andrzej Chodkjewicz's
study before the 1978 New South Wales state election found that significant
sections of the Sydney Turkish community who were entitled to vote were
unenrolled.[19] William Bostock, in 1975, wrote that most people would accept
that liberal democracy finds a very secure place in Australia today.[20] Yet
Chodkjewicz's Sydney studies suggest that migrants are greatly disadvantaged in
the political process. Lorna Lippmann also suggests that non-English speaking
groups are functionally disadvantaged at vital times, such as before the Law, in
illness or accident, in obtaining schooling or job training, and in employment.[21]

If we are to do our job as rhetors, we must ensure that governments provide
more than lip-service to democratic ideals. While it is not the job of rhetors as
teachers to teach a politically partisan set of values, it is important to help
students consider the needs and consequences of their actions in society.
Democratic education is the purposive development of students who are active,
informed, curious, and capable contributors to the development of society, and
language teachers share a significant responsibility in this development.

It is likely that integrating an approach such as occurs at QIT will allow the
teacher to become, as W.J. Crocker suggests, "more purposeful and effective in
helping… students to develop their skills of oral communication."[22] Yet the
rhetorical canon[23] is a vital component of such an approach, since it provides the

teacher with the resource for viewing language in its social (that is, cultural/political/people-oriented) context. Rhetors may well *be* the democratic process.

NOTE: Revised version of a paper, "Developing Oral Communication in a Pluralistic Society: Rhetors and the Democratic Process," shared at the 1979 Conference on Developing Oral Communication, University of New England, Armidale NSW, July 15 and subsequently published with permission in Crocker, W.J. (Ed) (1980), *Developing Oral Communication Competence*, Armidale, NSW: The University of New England, pp 85-91

References

1. An aphorism from a USA postage stamp, indicating the sustained concern with oral communication as an integral part of the democratic process.
2. Halloran, S.M. (1975), "On the End of Rhetoric: Classical and Modern," *College English*, February, 36(6), p. 621
3. Stenhouse, Lawrence (1967), *Culture and Education*, London: Nelson, quoted in Ipswich State High School English Curriculum Guide, Ipswich, Qld, Australia
4. Scanlan, Ross (1961), "The Nazi Rhetorician," in Howes, Raymond F. (Ed.), *Historical Studies of Rhetoric and Rhetoricians,* Ithaca: Cornell University Press, pp. 352-65
5. Hymes, D. (1975), "On Communication Competence," excerpts in Pride, J.B. and J. Holmes (Eds.), *Sociolinguistics: Selected Readings*, Harmondsworth: Penguin, p. 269-93
6. Wilkinson, A. (1971), *Foundations of Language: Talking and Reading in Young Children*, London: Oxford University Press, p. 96
7. Grey, A. (n.d.), "Who is Literate?" *Literacy Discussion*, 7(2), p. 43
8. For a comprehensive but now dated survey on these matters, see Levin, Murray B. (1962), "Political Strategy for the Alienated Voter," *Public Opinion Quarterly*, 26, p. 49
9. McLellan, David (1978), "Political Theory," in Inglis, Fred *Literature and Environment*, in Crick, Bernard and Alex Porter (Eds.), *Political Education and Political Literacy*, London: Longman, p. 167
10. McLellan, p. 167
11. Ingram, D.E. (1976), "Something There Is That Doesn't Love a Wall: Current Developments in Foreign Language Teaching," *Audio Visual Language Journal*, 14(2), pp. 71-85
12. Ingram, p. 77
13. Ingram, p. 77
14. Courts, D.C. Head, English, Churchlands CAE, communication with author
15. For non-Australian readers, "ocker" is Australian slang for: a boorish person, a person aggressively Australian in speech and behavior, often for humorous effect. (*Australian Pocket Oxford Dictionary)*
16. Clarke, Marcus (1877), "A Tall, Coarse, Strong-jawed, Greedy, Pushing, Talented Man," quoted in Turner, Ian (Ed.), *The Australian Dream,* Melbourne: Sun, pp. 132-3

17. Ingram, D.E. (1978), "Education for Pluralism: The Changing Role of Language Teaching in Australia," Ingram, D.E. and T.J. Quinn (Eds.), *Language Learning in Australia*, Melbourne: Australian International, p. 74

18. McKinnon, K.R. (Chairman) (1978), *Report for the Triennium 1979-81*, Canberra: Schools Commission, p. 108

19. Interview with researcher, A. Chodkjewicz, October 11, 1978. Also, Chodkjewicz, Andrezej (1978), *Political Communication: Turkish Community in Sydney*, Author's private collection, p. 7 [in Australia, enrolment to vote and voting are compulsory]

20 Bostock, William W. (1975), "The Linguistic and Cultural Bases for Australian Democracy," *Plural Societies*, [The Hague], Winter, 6(4), p. 73

21. Lippmann, Lorna (1976), "Literacy and Ethnic Minorities in Australia," *Literacy Discussion*, Summer, 7(2), p. 23

22. Crocker, W.J. (1979), "Approaches to the Teaching of Oral Communication," Conference on Developing Oral Communication Competence, University of New England and Armidale College of Advanced Education, Armidale NSW, July, p. 9

23. Crocker, W.J. (1977), "Teaching Oracy in the English Programme," *English in Australia*, February, 39, pp. 54-8, for discussion on the integrative teaching of rhetorical principles

2: Rhetoric of Democracy

...truthful, lawful, and just speech

— Isocrates

Media presenters on public affairs television in Australia are caught in a constant battle against restrictive aspects of station policy guidelines, diminishing budgets, limited time, variable staff talent, and other limits to challenge effectiveness. It is not surprising perhaps that media presenters in this country have taken little opportunity to date to obtain information about the effectiveness or otherwise of their own work to enhance the understanding of information.

The growing field of researchers studying communication may offer the necessary knowledge here, but it remains to be shown whether media practitioners will make use of such insight concerning their own activities. In contrast, in some Scandinavian countries, media management have actively sought the integration of academic researchers as program advisors, to get a better understanding of a range of programming needs–including the effectiveness of certain programs in reaching target markets and of the likely effect of certain program series and a station's programming practices on community beliefs about their own society.

Lacking such information about themselves, media presenters are as unqualified as many members of the community to claim the role of enlarging people's knowledge of their society. As a result, Australia's most frequent mass communicators have acted out improvised roles, potentially adding credence to the proposition that "culture and communication are irreconcilably opposed."[1] It is commonplace to note that the mass media, and especially the electronic media, are significant influences on a society's cultural values and self-knowledge. The communication techniques that our children learn from their electronic baby-sitters are built on the dubious bases of standardized opinions and tastes, commercial advertising, impersonalized and conformist lifestyles, and even manipulation of minds and information that vigorously mitigates against people's critical faculties and the originality of their creative capacity. If the communication techniques of future generations are based on such assumptions, we will witness the continued disappearance of "what we consider most profound and most significant in what we call our culture."[2]

This paper briefly comments on these issues by examining some aspects of how mass media in Australia are involved in information sharing and argues that the character of this process is central to democratic government. The paper notes that public figures' use of the key symbol "democracy" and democratic assumptions to frame public talk is a key part of the context in which people use information. Two types of information user are briefly sketched. It is suggested that neither the needs of these users nor the claims or presumptions of mass media commentators and public figures asserting democracy can be satisfied where democratic principles are paid little more than lip service. The paper is in every sense political, since public discussion even of the central concern of this symposium, namely scientific matters, necessarily conforms to the norms and requirements of political communication.

Scientific experts, social activists, politicians, other public figures, and journalists continuously discuss the formation of government policy and the day-to-day administration of the country's affairs from a general assumption that we live in a free society. Some merely praise the existence of this society, while others use the popular idea of democracy and its assumed presence to evaluate government and opposition proposals, policies, or actions. Democracy is a common reference point for much public communication.

But what democracy is and how media presenters in so many vastly different political systems—from a Western capitalist nation to a welfare state to a dictatorship—can all seek to characterize themselves as democratic are touched upon in this paper. The meanings of democracy in popular usage are varied and the confusion of these meanings is one way in which public figures obfuscate events and information. The paper mentions some ways that Australian public figures characterize their actions as democratic, but similar processes are at work in other Western democracies.

In a society such as Australia, which is ostensibly free from great inequalities and espouses "mateship" and egalitarianism as part of its national ethos, the many references to democracy by social commentators and Australian politicians might be expected. This reliance on references to a "free society" to find common ground with audiences, however, is hardly unique. In the United Kingdom, as Brian Groombridge commented, "...democracy provides the official ideology and the rhetoric of our society…"[3] Frequently media presenters define individual freedom as a selfless dedication to higher democratic aims, and in many circumstances pay lip service to its strength, while advocating policies which might erode areas of its free operation.[4]

The key symbol "democracy" is the framework for much public persuasion. To understand the methods used by Australian public figures to persuade the community of policy proposals, it is necessary to evaluate the process by which public figures have employed and confused meanings of democracy. It is also necessary to review the process by which these usages of the word set values and influence the community's perceptions of both the system of government and public figures themselves.

The concept of democracy has a long association with communication. Aristotle prescribed that for democracy to exist a state's citizens must be informed, curious, and capable speakers.[5] Other classical writers assumed that effective speaking by good people was a basic prerequisite for the democratic state, and more recently press freedom is one tradition that is overtly and often vigorously defended in the United States and other Western countries. Press freedom is claimed to be essential to the continuance of democracy as a system of government.

Up to the middle of the twentieth century, Walter Lippmann was a foremost proponent of the press as the "Indispensable Opposition."[6] UNESCO has focused its efforts through its Committee on Communication to examine the world information order and sought to develop a more representative network for the dissemination of world news than the present system, so dominated by the sectional interests of the major news services based mainly in the United States, United Kingdom, and France. Implicitly, such discussions imply that when everyone can gain access to competing ideas, opinions, and information in a free marketplace of ideas, then democracy will flourish.[7]

The narrowness of this proposal, which implies that free discussion means full discussion should as often as needed be challenged. While it is important for people to have access to full information on matters of concern, it is equally important that:

1) individuals develop a capacity to critically discuss often conflicting and complex information, and

2) information be available as far as possible without the influences of selectivity or distortion from journalists' or other gatekeepers' views coming between information sources and the community.

Studies have shown that personal conviction distorts the reasoning process, that prejudice precludes persuasion, and that people do not employ reasonableness as the basis for accepting or rejecting arguments.[8] The old ideal relationship of a public citizen standing before an audience openly informing

10

them of issues, actions, or occurrences, and seeking or leading debate, if it ever existed, can hardly be said to exist today. Now, the public figure's research officer, speech writer, the public figure, news services, journalists, news editors, and even proprietors of media organizations can all introduce elements of personal filtering or censorship, directly or through others on their behalf. Consequently, it is perhaps rarely in the modern state that a "full" message is a complete message, free of filtering, distortion, or worse.

Philosophers have claimed that a society cannot long remain free while its sources of ideas are in chains,[9] with propaganda often the most appropriate descriptor of public talk directed at limiting understandings or discussion. The French philosopher, Jacques Ellul, noted that freedom is everywhere proclaimed but that it is only freedom to tell the established and consecrated truth.[10]

Public figures in Australia regularly seek to elevate their actions by associating their advocacy with the respected liberal democratic tradition—at the very least to establish rapport with an audience. Just two examples from speeches of two articulate Australia prime ministers show how, even on nonpartisan occasions, this will be done. Both are from addresses to the National Press Club in Washington DC. Firstly, The Hon E. G. Whitlam in 1975:

> So in accepting your invitation for a second time, I again pay tribute to the manifest and enduring strength of the democracy of the United States, of which the press is so fundamental a part.[11]

Secondly, The Rt Hon R. G. Menzies in 1955:

> Now let me make it perfectly clear that I am a Prime Minister of a democratic country and in my country, Prime Ministers don't go wandering around the world offering new policies off their own hook.[12]

It is not only with the American press, however, that these and other public figures rely on references to democracy.

Such comments, though brief and benign, do nonetheless extend a fundamental assumption that each speaker is the essential truth-giver. In reality, of course, truth in public talk can range from a context-setting reassurance, as here, through to lip-service or, worse still, to distortions. Even if people recognize that a truth that they are being presented with is really half-truth, limited truth, or truth out of context, key questions will remain concerning the extent to which listeners will step with a clarity of purpose among emotive ambiguities.

Ellul has also pointed out the hazard of major sources of information continuously presenting the same assumptions in messages.[13] When the channels of communication are effectively monopolized by whatever means, as John Meaney noted in describing Nazi Germany, people will gradually, unconsciously,

11

even unwillingly accept quite crazy suggestions as disagreeable at first and then eventually believe in them.[14]

When this translates to autonomic actions in relation to elections, for example, freedom is at best an inaccurate description of a procedure whereby people regularly make their way to the ballot box unaware of the real basis for their decision, and without the capacity to make free decision. Democracies, Ellul claims,[15] have been fed on the idea that truth may be hidden for a while but will triumph in the end, and that truth itself carries an explosive force. John Milton, of course, had proposed a similar view much earlier.

The perpetual puffery of public figures eager for the support of citizens induces a major and inevitable simplification and distortion of the complex issues affecting a modern state. This process is especially distorting when the basic premise of the liberal democratic tradition, that representatives are openly elected under conditions of free speech,[16] becomes lip service. Plato criticized democratic rhetoric as self-serving careerism that takes advantage of a gullible citizenry, and Herbert Marcuse insisted on a democracy that is not a mere coverup for domination.[17]

"Political language," in the famous polemic of George Orwell, "is designed to make lies sound truthful and murder respectable."[18] But if, as I have suggested earlier, people judge political events from the reports of electronic media, newspapers, or politicians themselves, they generally have few real guidelines for assessing the value of such reports. Increasingly, in Australia as in some other Western industrialized nations, we are subject often both to information overload and information deficiency. Both effects mean we might rarely be well informed. As noted earlier, half-truth and especially truth out of context are the stock in trade of public communication. In commenting on this effect, Ellul further argued that the most propagandized people in the community are the most "educated, intelligent" individuals, because they:

1) absorb the largest amount of second-hand information,
2) feel a compelling need to have an opinion, and
3) consider themselves capable of "judging."[19]

Within the broader community too, but most notably within this "educated, intelligent" group, we increasingly witness the evolution of two human types that predominate in the social information landscape—and you might like to consider whether either of these describes how you feel at times.

The official biological names for these types are ***Vacuus Informationi*** and ***Delusus Informationi.***

The first, ***Vacuus Informationi,*** is the being who operates in an information vacuum. This person knows that something incorrect is in some file somewhere but doesn't know how to find out about it—whatever it is. Yearning for knowledge from official files, in frustration, this person, as a change from pursuing government information, might even confront a bank manager or accountant to distil personal information like some ratings of financial reputation not currently available. Invariably, this person is met at first diplomatically, but progressively less so, and feels frustrated wandering the corridors of government departments, seeking the ever-elusive department information officer. The extreme personification of this type is chronically frustrated and fears all silence as evidence of conspiracy.

The second, **Delusus Informationi,** represents a type well known to all but themselves. This is the lean, frequently organizationally savvy person, once hungry for paper to push, but increasingly content with technological devices to satisfy a lust for achieving that highest, but most unattainable of aims, "the state of being informed." This being wants to know every detail of the mountains of material that pass by everyone in a day. Extreme manifestations of this type might take the form of a research scientist, or reference librarian, or academic, believing that being so well-read, with subscriptions to the more informative and respected news media, like *The Bulletin, The Financial Review,* or *The Australian,* as well as specialized journals and magazines, that surely this person is the most "absorbing," "opinion-giving," carefully judging person anyone could know.

Sadly, both creatures, whose continued evolution we haven't time to track, become converted to the belief, perhaps assisted by the surrounding assurances from the high-toned assumptions of the democratic debate in the public media, that they are powerless to act other than as they do. They likely remain victims of propaganda and soon lose what critical ability they once had, or totally restrict these capacities to their professional activities. They will avoid exposure to representatives of the media, because of the potential for conflict, volatility, or just plain unfair treatment, and feel happiest responding to polemic and invective directed against their favorite punching-bag in the shadow-play of political debate on the television screen.

Using hyperbole on that screen, public figures enlarge their own power in the political process, and neither media interviewers nor the audience requires much accounting for or outline of real evidence to support assertions. Stanley Kelley sketched such developments in American political campaigning, writing that:

> Campaign communication is filled with evasions, distortions, ambiguities, irrelevancies, and calculated efforts to mislead. Seemingly, it confirms the proposition that the rational interests of candidates and parties lead them to encourage irrationality in the electorate.[20]

Kelley seems to presuppose that only rationality is required, reflecting a common social assumption, shared by some critics or commentators, to advocate "facts" rather than "values" as the appropriate concern for public debate. But the tension between emotional versus factual content of speech might be less important than understanding the language of the stronger emotions–such as recognizing what commentary is just driven by prejudice. This is the language of imperatives. For example, name-calling, as a commonly used device of the propagandist, is an imperative that the listener should regard the subject so named in a specific way. Likewise, polemic is used to attack others, usually to win by compelling submission. The propagandist seeking compulsion to imperatives makes so-called communication more akin to Meaney's notion of psychical coercion[21] than free discussion.

Unlike the educator, the propagandist is especially powerful when using polemic, to deny free thought and seek submission to a restricted view of a culture–ordinarily with the precondition that anyone under the sway of propaganda will strongly believe in the success or status of the propagandist. The process will be most developed in dictatorships, where the specter of permanent crisis and alleged external threat is made so great that the dictator can convince followers that freedom of expression is subversive of national survival.[22] Modern Western political campaigns, using many of the same processes as the propaganda campaigns of dictatorships, also show similarity in their use of political language in ways that George Orwell observed. Significant differences distinguishing such campaigns will largely be found in the intent of the public figure.

Effective propaganda in all societies is based on the principle that:

> What people believe about the future shapes their responses to present events–these beliefs about the future build a structure of expectations.[23]

And the purpose of the propagandist using the mass media is to create a person clinging …to clear certainties… assimilated into uniform groups and wanting it that way.[24] Clearly this is antithetical to any original nature of democratic society. It is scarcely adequate any longer to excuse individuals paying lip service to democracy, whatever the purpose. It is dysfunctional to democracy to allow such appeals to be unchallenged. In our own state of Queensland, one writer has suggested that the government minority party has so gerrymandered the electoral boundaries and made such persistent appeals to institutional authority that the public accepts the party's senior status in government, feeling secure that the party's "socialistic initiatives" are in the voters' interests and promote "private enterprise"[25]–for quite the alphabet soup of conflicting political stances. Bystanders in a democracy need to get critically involved and be more aware members of the community if democracy is to continue.

Regrettably, some media commentators trade in the processes of propaganda, disseminating unmoderated polemical claims word-for-word, spreading what are readily recognizable as propaganda devices like name-calling, false disjunction, scapegoat, or the "big lie."[26] To the non-critical consumer of such news stories, this kind of reporting at a surface level appears to conform to a news norm of recording events or statements "objectively," or in a "balanced" way. Yet, sensational content disseminated without moderation not only irresponsibly lifts the profile of the reporter but, more significantly, helps to white-ant genuine public debate, debilitating democracy further.

When the processes that public figures use to convert social and political circumstances to their own purposes are too little scrutinized, informed debate is no longer possible. An essential characteristic of democracy is the opportunity for community members to make informed interrogation of political statements.[27] When this is denied, democracy becomes a sham. A community is then obliged to live by norms and values everywhere proclaimed that are at best mythical.

These processes of building a democratic myth render our two information-yearning citizens *Vacuus Informationi* and *Delusus Informationi* powerless. Amid a flood of misleading and contradictory information available to them, they are constantly reassured that all will be well—that Orwell's 1984 will never be, but that in our community we practice "Goodspeak,"[28] as any democracy should. And, while it's not perfect, it's not that bad. Are you reassured? Is there nothing you can do? What will you do?

NOTE: Revised version of a paper, "Rhetoric of Democracy: Communication and the Politics of Information," shared at the 1980 Conference on Public Information, held at Queensland Institute of Technology, Brisbane, Australia, subsequently published with permission in Ward, W.T. and M.M. Bryden (Eds.) (1981), *Public Information: Your Right to Know*, St. Lucia, Qld: Royal Society of Queensland, pp. 15-20

Acknowledgment

With appreciation to D. Brosnan, Classics Department, The University of Queensland, for his assistance in the invention of the two biological names used in this paper.

References

1. Olea, V.F. (n.d.), *Culture and Communication*, International Commission for the Study of Communication Problems, Document No. 75, Paris: UNESCO
2. Olea
3. Groombridge, Brian (1972), *Television and the People: A Programme for Democratic Participation*, Harmondsworth: Penguin
4. Dean, R.L. (1955), "Aspects of Persuasive Appeal in Stevenson's Campaign Speeches," *The Speaker*, May, p. 21
5. Carleton, W.G. (1951), "Effective Speech in a Democracy," *Southern Speech Journal*, 17, pp. 2-13

6. Lippmann, Walter (1960), "The Indispensable Opposition," in Eastman, A.M., and others (Eds.), *The Norton Reader*, New York: Norton

7. Chaffee, S.H. (1975), *Political Communication: Issues and Strategies for Research*, Thousand Oaks, CA: Sage

8. Clevenger, T. (1960), "Speaker and Society: The Role of Freedom in a Democratic State," *Southern Speech Journal*, 26, pp. 93-9

9. Clevenger

10. Ellul, Jacques (1973), *The New Demons*, New York: Seabury

11. Menzies, Robert G. (1955), *Address to the National Press Club*, Washington DC, March 16

12. Whitlam, E. Gough (1975), *Address to the National Press Club*, Washington DC, May 8

13. Ellul, Jacques (1965), *Propaganda: The Formation of Men's Attitudes*, New York: Vintage

14. Meaney, J.W. (1951), "Propaganda as Psychical Coercion," *Review of Politics*, 13, pp. 64-87

15. Ellul (1965)

16. Williams, Raymond (1976), *Keywords: A Vocabulary of Culture and Society*, London: Fontana

17. Bay, Christian (1977), "Human Needs and Political Education," in Fitzgerald, R. (Ed.), *Human Needs and Politics*, Sydney: Pergamon

18. Orwell, George (1981), "Politics and the English Language," in *A Collection of Essays*, Orlando, FL: Harvest, p. 170

19. Kellen, Konrad (1965), "Introduction" to Jacques Ellul's *Propaganda: The Formation of Men's Attitudes*, p. vi

20. Kelley, S. (1960), *Political Campaigning: Problems in Creating an Informed Electorate*, Washington DC: Brookings Institution

21. Meaney

22. Fagen, R. (1966), *Politics and Communication*, Boston: Little Brown

23. Lerner, D. (1972), "Effective Propaganda," in Lerner, D. (Ed.), *Propaganda in War and Crisis*, New York: Arno

24. Ellul (1965)

25. Wells, D. (1979), *The Deep North*, Collingwood, Vic: Outback

26. Brown, J.A.C. (1963), *Techniques of Persuasion: From Propaganda to Brainwashing*, Harmondsworth: Pelican

27. Carleton, W.G. (1951), "Effective Speech in a Democracy," *Southern Speech Journal*, 17, pp. 2-13

28. Orwell, George (1954), "Principles of Newspeak," *Nineteen Eighty-Four*, Harmondsworth: Penguin, pp. 241-51

3: Developing the Culture of Trust

Trust is the lubrication that makes it possible for organizations to work.

– Warren G. Bennis

Times of financial, economic, or social instability or threat heighten the attention of the media and all of us to questions of trust. Major corporate scandals, like Enron and WorldCom, or an economic meltdown like 2008, or scandals of financial mismanagement in nonprofit organizations spawn news articles, along with a flurry of new surveys of opinion. Organizations seeking to reassure stakeholders launch vigorous efforts to understand and enhance levels of trust, searching out ways to repackage recipes for regaining trust. Much of this is situation-specific guidance in the aftermath of each destabilization.

Practical studies or guidance concerning trust and its relation to communication principles and techniques have also appeared in articles over many years, in publications like *Corporate Communications: An International Journal.* Observations of the PR Coalition[1] and individual papers[2] have offered further ways to think about specific challenges. A special report of the Business Roundtable for Corporate Ethics and the Arthur W. Page Society called on business leaders to install enterprise values, build relations with mediating organizations, embrace transparency, work within one's own business sector to build trust, and commit to enhancing contributions to society.[3] In early 2010, the International Association of Business Communicators commissioned a study that recommended businesses focus on the drivers of trust, which were described as competence, openness and honesty, concern for employees and stakeholders, reliability, and the identification of individual goals within the organization.[4]

While the specific impact of such offerings to enhance trust is difficult to assess, an opinion survey firm in 2009 issued its report on overall trends, "Trust in corporations down around the world…[the] % who trust corporations **less** this year: 62% Global, 77% U.S., 67% U.K., 67% France, 73% Germany, 56% China, 49% India…" among informed publics aged 25-64 in 20 countries.[5] In 2010, the same firm reported "Global trust in business is up modestly but the rebound is fueled by a spike in a handful of Western countries, especially the United States where it jumped 18 points to 54 percent."[6] Alongside the expectation for improving trust, the lessons of the decades are clear–for all the efforts to build trust through public discourse, board and senior management commitments, training programs, advertising programs, employee relations efforts, opinion surveys, extolling successes, and so many, many sincere attempts to build trust, monitors such as the Edelman surveys demonstrate that any real momentum in a right direction is yet to be accomplished through such efforts. Why is this so?

The lack of success fits with one observation about recipes for management success in general, "…the everyday rate of any real success on the part of managers and executives seems to bear no correlation to the exponential flood of advice about 'how to succeed.'"[7] Within the finance sector and beyond, during economic meltdown, as well as before and since, the demands on leaders and other communicators to become chefs of an instant pudding of trust keep growing in number and complexity. While the recipes for building trust bring much convergence of thought, trust is driven less by reason or behaviors than by emotion.

This paper invites consideration of some different ways to view stakeholders' lack of trust in an organization and suggests a different approach to the problem. For consistency within the context of the concrete actions noted above,[8] the paper suggests an approach for engaging stakeholders. The steps suggested are to help identify organizational values, to build relationships based on trust with mediating organizations, to embrace transparency, to execute more considered communications, and to make necessary adjustments that help build the levels of trust needed for large-scale gains. The paper draws on the published studies of some better documented areas of stakeholder relations, such as employee communication and crisis communication. In conclusion, some operating principles and tools are suggested that might assist an individual organization's development and ongoing testing for progress in building stakeholder trust.

Developing New Patterns of Communication

A compulsive impulse of a variety of organizations is to use image advertising as a tool to regain legitimacy, with a wide variety of approaches. The most basic efforts seek to renew relationships based on an organization's presumed competence. Using a corpus of 74 print advertisements, one study of the advertisements of international corporate banks and financial institutions noted "an overwhelming focus in both text and images on recounting achievements and competencies at the expense of providing assurance of their integrity, truthfulness or attention to clients' needs."[9] In early 2010, the ambitiously ambiguous Nike television advertisement, with its voice-over from the deceased father of Tiger Woods, attracted a short media and industry buzz of speculation about its processes and effectiveness.[10] Also, Toyota faced a difficult series of vehicle recalls and blistering public commentary in early 2010, and the company's advertising in the United States made much of thanking loyal customers, to present role models for others to follow.

With public discourse expected to continue at a high pitch, with stakeholder-cautiousness evident, with investors, donors, or clients/customers especially sensitive about the quality of services or products an organization provides, and with staff satisfaction often low, the importance of establishing communications beyond the one-way messaging of advertising to build trust with stakeholders cannot be overstated. Developing a culture of trust has been long recognized as enabling large-scale gains. In classical times, it was the good citizen (*rhetor*) who empowered public discourse, with sensitivity to a variety of perspectives in the audience, very substantially through the appeal of *ethos* or character. Character and reputation are no less important now, when the endless news cycle, social media, and community gossip make the contemporary world more like "being aboard a careering juggernaut…rather than being in a carefully controlled and well-driven motor car."[11] The communication of qualities to encourage trust with stakeholders has an ever-growing importance, which requires new self-awareness and the recognition of new patterns, as well as new skills.

For anyone seeking a future different from the past, the focus still needs to be by engaging with values that are valued and expressed by people both inside and outside organizations, individually and collectively. Ongoing, a catalytic role for organizational leaders interacting with stakeholders is called for, rather than just dictating an organizational values statement as a top-down manifesto. The common sense and understanding of an organization's stakeholders are powerful resources to engage—and how communication is established will determine what gains accrue from efforts to engender trust.

Establish Common Values

Stakeholders recognize early in communication whether someone is genuine about their interests. Values embedded in communication will signal how much a stakeholder is valued. When the goal of communication is just to "get a message out," stakeholders understand intuitively that their views, feelings, or perspectives are not considered important, regardless of how much these might be pandered to. Building mutual understanding ordinarily requires an ebb-and-flow of conversation, or at least some sense of it, where participants acknowledge and indicate mutual appreciation. An organization seeking to build trust with stakeholders might require a substantial reset in its current approaches to communication.

For example, the annual report to stakeholders is one stylized communication, acknowledged by some to be a statement that "communicates with individual shareholders and seeks to create good impressions and build confidence... [but] ...is primarily a one-way exchange."[11] Many efforts are increasingly ensuring that annual reports of corporations, government, and nonprofit organizations report against previously stated goals, as performance reports. This at least suggests some symbolic commitment to accountability. But too many annual reports and other organizational communication, especially video and glossy publications, will generate feelings at the wrong end of the skepticism or cynicism scales.

Communications inherently suggesting command and control approaches tend to work poorly to build trust in most situations. Advocates of these approaches really need to recognize the irony that Shannon and Weaver's transmission theory of message transfer, so many decades ago, was to explain how "white noise" in the telephone wire interfered with the message transmission and what was heard.[12] This information transfer model was never intended to be wisdom's guide to effective communication–which is characterized by more nuanced human concerns, like understanding in the sense of mutual appreciation and trust. Given what is known about the variety of meanings different people give to the same words and how human beings construct meaning from a variety of cues, it is vital that organizational communication be less didactic and more interactive in purpose and reality.

The importance for leaders to build relationships with stakeholders is becoming more generally acknowledged, with "the role of the leader as a listener, communicator and educator... [now] ...imperative in formulating and facilitating a positive organizational culture."[13] When communications are conceived in these terms throughout an organization, improved understandings might be accomplished, but this quality should not be confined to one-on-one communication. An effective speech, advertisement, or other communication to a wide audience builds trust by resonating with "the common history of the relationship, ... coloured by current expectations about the future."[14]

Anyone within an organization is positioned to be an exemplar of communication values that are genuinely interactive. Whether through strategic planning, issues management, media relations outreach, employee communications, or a plethora of granular communication activities, work colleagues who incline to interactive communication have a special role in the evolution of trust. What is often advocated for nonprofit organizations in the new economy is to bring each stakeholder group into contact with pertinent areas of the organization, to encourage genuine engagement. The purpose is to stimulate participation of stakeholders in developing new ideas to address community needs, which is a potentially powerful mode of engagement[15] for any organization. Techniques of issues management can be directly applied to help shape this approach, although it is important to step beyond the "...traditional ...issues management where organisations 'decide' on their plans, 'dictate' them to stakeholders, and prepare their 'defence', ...[which]...will no longer be adequate."[16]

A piece of good news for communicators in the bad news about the level of trust that stakeholders might have for an organization is the opportunity this provides to adjust communication values, expectations, and practices. Suggestions to assist with this effort abound, such as attending to the "...nine roles of communication, including cultural conscience, interpreter of ethics, facilitator of re-visioning and openness, and communication planner."[17] To deal with multiple and sometimes conflicting ethical frameworks likely to emerge in such efforts, teachers and advocates concerned with developing an ethical basis to persuasive practice have long disseminated workable approaches.[18] Continuous review is recommended to refresh approaches and ensure that communication is responsive, responsible, and nuanced to the needs, wants, and perceptions of stakeholders.

As the complexities of the communication landscape continue to increase, the importance of developing a practical understanding of the values implicit within communication practice will also keep increasing. For example, one study's "...data analyses showed that all ten principles of authentic communication were correlated with communication success."[19] What remains a constant is that whether communication is perceived as authentic will determine whether there is communication for understanding.

Motivate Trust

It is recognized that in any organization's communications, stakeholder protection, trust or confidence, value, respect, and satisfaction are dominant themes and values.[20] Experiences from employee relations efforts can be directly applicable to exploring the complexities of motivation and what works to build trust. Best practices for interaction with employees can provide useful approaches to consider for other stakeholder groups. Of course, different factors motivate people in different situations. But for employees as well as more generally, outcomes such as accountability, adaptability, alignment, collaboration, leadership, and trust will only be leveraged through appeals to motivators such as safety, growth, accomplishment, belonging, and purpose–

which are the powerful emotional drivers within people.[21] When it comes to the development of intrinsic motivators, three guidelines are to:

- Develop powerful values.
- Connect with people to produce a sense of belonging.
- Constantly articulate purpose.[22]

It is the "why" value of an organization that engages people internal or external to it. While this value ought to be found expressed in the mission, too often mission statements are really goal statements articulating what the corporation does. If a corporation does not have a compelling statement of why it exists, putting attention on the expression of a "why value" is a way to strengthen engagement with stakeholders. Everyone accepts that an organization's goal will be to make money or deliver a service, and so on, but "what does it exist for?"[23] is what will interest stakeholders.

A simple step to clarify the value of why an organization exists is to put this question to stakeholders who already value it. Following up with conversation about what would be missing if the organization ceased to exist will ordinarily be not only revealing, but also often have the effect of increasing stakeholder engagement. This approach can identify worthwhile and unexpected answers to help shape a statement of organizational values that aligns with stakeholders' beliefs and values. Additionally, when stakeholders have helped to evolve an organization's values statement, some will be willing to help "spread the word" on these values, inside the organization and/or in the community—with the added power, by implication, of a testimonial.

Engagement Bridges

In the new economy, iterative engagement with stakeholders and a capacity to build a mutuality of interests will be increasingly important and might prove to be one of the few true determiners of organizational strength. It is hard to think of a circumstance in the business, government, or nonprofit sectors where building such bridges will ever be other than increasingly important. The good news is that when organizations communicate more effectively with stakeholders, this opens access to a wider array of the interpersonal-cum-mass communication vehicles of social networks, to provide the ongoing interaction many stakeholders expect. It is certainly true that "…for companies in the twenty-first century, the creation of value increasingly depends on intangible assets, such as knowledge, systems, data, intellectual property, brands and market relationships."[24] Substantial changes in the outlook and methods of many organizations will be increasingly required to recognize the centrality of such intangible assets, much less to sustain commitment to aspects of communication that stakeholders consider core rather than ancillary to an organization's function.

The challenges to planning and executing substantial change of course should be carefully considered ahead of any action. Estimates suggest that up to 70 % of change efforts fail.[25] An interesting analysis of the forces working against change has concluded that "If an organization prepares inadequately for change, resistance emerges, organizational inertia thrives, and the efforts to change fail."[26] Obviously, a core concern is to sufficiently consider pertinent features of the culture of the organization, to search for what might be the largest drivers in an organization's readiness for change.[27]

To have much potential for success, changes to communication approaches and practices must be developed in consultation with people throughout the organization, attentive to their perceptions of cultural realities. It is also important to remember that "extraordinary achievements carry more risk of failure...Most people look askance at those who take great risks, or make great efforts, or discipline themselves severely. Until one of them succeeds. Then people pretend not only that they were certain all along of that person's achievement, but they are then willing to buy fan t-shirts or other paraphernalia to identify themselves with the achiever."[28]

Preparing for Change

The changes to how an organization approaches communication already suggested in this paper will be major undertakings for some organizations, and preparation is required. A first step is to analyze both the organizational culture and current communications. A tool to show "hot spots" in the organizational culture that might block optimal success is *The Organizational Vital Signs*, which its developers present as a statistically reliable assessment against norms.[29] The five climate factors addressed are:

- Accountability and Responsibility
- Collaboration and Problem Solving
- Perception of Leadership
- Alignment to the Mission
- Adaptability for Change

–plus, an overlay dimension of Trust. For the assessment of communication flow and effectiveness, instruments developed by the International Association for Business Communicators and the PR Council might prove helpful. It is important though to be careful of overkill before administering such instruments, since considering ways to adjust communication approaches might be as simple as making a content and tone analysis of a selection of oral and written communications. Certainly, any analyses and assessments should enable

23

thoughtful shaping of the philosophy, goals, skills, and commitments that are required to maximize success.

Factors that will affect the change efforts need to be anticipated and will include aspects of communication from the points of view of both the external stakeholders and employees, such as levels and types of "…information, feelings of belonging to a community, and feelings of uncertainty, ... [that] …have an influence on resistance to change, [and] … will affect the effectiveness of the change effort."[30] Experience with employee communication programs also highlight the need for stakeholder communication to consider "…the communicative competencies of middle managers and their capacity to enter into dialogue…"[31] Decision will be needed about the designation of who is to sustain organizational contact with stakeholders. Assigning and coordinating relationship managers requires sensitivity to whom among management are best suited for the key role of coordinating and mentoring colleagues who engage stakeholders. Given that this effort will need to be sustained through more rather than a limited number of interfaces, sound understandings of the communication competencies of an organization's people to perform these roles will be key.

Mediating Relationships

In addition to reaching out to stakeholder groups directly, building relationships with a variety of organizations to reach stakeholders can also help tremendously. For example, in the United States and internationally, engineering, aerospace, pharmaceutical, and other manufacturing companies have built relationships with nonprofit organizations, by contributing to the conduct of robotics or other hi-tech competitions designed to inspire youth to pursue science, technology, engineering, or math-based careers. Companies participating in such partnerships provide technology professionals as mentors and sponsor competing teams, thereby reaching to children, parents, teachers, and media very widely.

Many nonprofit organizations enjoy continuous growth in approval and trust from the communities they serve, at times when trust in corporations is not generally increasing. Absent any further widespread nonprofit mismanagement scandals, opportunities will keep growing for corporations to benefit from appropriate relationships with nonprofit organizations. Likewise, nonprofit organizations can benefit from a compatible fit with a corporation, including increased reach into a community. Nonprofit organizations have well defined needs, such as additional sources of funds, access to networks of corporate leaders, profile and relationship within communities, or *pro bono* expertise. Such needs are doorways to find ways to build relationships, with the dynamics of these interactions varying greatly. But by ensuring clarity up-front between the

24

most senior management of the participating corporation and the nonprofit organization about expectations and mutual actions, relationships can be well understood, valued, and continuously strengthened.

Unexpected benefits often come through these arrangements. For example, sharing understandings about the sophisticated relationship management systems used in the partnering organizations can be a treasure-trove to enhance each partner's systems. Such information sharing and interaction can provide opportunity to refine more robust systems in both types of organization.

Both a corporation and a nonprofit organization can benefit from systematically reviewing the landscape of a wide range of corporations and nonprofit organizations in local, national, and international areas of operation. Locating a match of aims, needs, or resources can enable affiliations or more formal agreements. In many countries and localities, the registration of nonprofit organizations continues to increase at record levels driving demand for quality board members, in addition to the enormous need for board members who add value to well-established nonprofit organizations.

Embrace Transparency

In the "juggernaut" ride of the new economy, it is the organization that discloses both negative and positive information that will stand out from others as more trustworthy. It seems clear "…from a communicative point of view, it might be wise to publish negative aspects as well as the positive ones to promote trust and corporate credibility."[32] This is widely understood from experiences in crisis communications, employee communications, and client/customer or stakeholder relations programs. In this context, the importance of plain language practices[33] also further increases for refining the nuances of communication. Within the wider community of stakeholders, as within any organization, genuine "straight talk" has potential for huge returns of goodwill and support.

However, "…the power of informal communication… [like] …the "rumor mill", should not be underestimated, and managers should not overestimate their own ability to control it."[34] For some organizations, the process of building trust might occur more like an ongoing crisis communication program for quite a while. Even the best intentions of a central communication function can be undercut or worse, when interfaces with stakeholders go awry.

It was found in a study of coordinated programs to transform organizations that "Communication during failed efforts seldom involves enough communication opportunities, lacks any sense of emerging identification, engenders distrust, and lacks productive humor. These problems are compounded by conflict avoidance and a lack of interpersonal communication skills. Members decouple the system, sheltering the existing culture until it is safe for it to reemerge later."[35] As with the communication of any sensitive concerns, judgment will be needed about when, what, and how to communicate.

It will be the CEO's lead that sets the significance and tone for all the organization's communications, whether for relations with employees or other stakeholders. How interactively the CEO communicates will be noticed and mirrored, so the CEO's responsibility for stakeholder engagement will always be substantial. The CEO will need to make strategic choices, such as to "...step up at the beginning of the crisis if the crisis pertains to organizational transgression or when the crisis becomes unbearable to organizational reputation. ... CEOs should refrain from stepping up at the height of the crisis."[36]

Steps to Be Best

With a lack of trust in corporations highlighted over many decades, it is doubtful that quick fixes, hype, or command and control message-sending might do more than reinforce existing beliefs, despite the sincerity underpinning efforts to build trust. Following the Enron and WorldCom debacles that will be long remembered, one observation was "More than seven in 10 Americans say they distrust CEOs of large corporations. Nearly eight in 10 believe that top executives of large companies will take 'improper actions' to help themselves at the expense of their companies."[37] Perhaps with more hope than evidence, another commentator at that time considered "The threat of jail time for those who are found guilty of deliberate misconduct may be just the ticket that's needed to force top executives to think before they engage in questionable practices..."[38] Not only do events since suggest this comment was wrong, the stain from failures in trust is not easily overcome in people's memory.

For corporations, government, or nonprofit organizations well into the future, the unavoidable truth will remain that "...many of the problems organisations are facing involve gaining legitimacy from stakeholders...[39] Accordingly, this paper proposes the following as some steps toward best practices for developing a culture of trust:

- Assess the current levels of trust within the organization and among stakeholders, by using instruments such as *The Organizational Vital Signs*.
- Engage stakeholders very closely to identify both why the organization is valued and what are the priorities of stakeholders— this also requires distilling and correlating the values common among stakeholders.
- Organize ongoing contact with stakeholders to evolve a sense of belonging.

26

- Articulate the organizational purpose constantly and consistently, from the CEO and throughout the organization.
- Build mediating relationships with other organizations, especially among trusted corporations and nonprofit organizations.
- Adopt pertinent principles of plain language and crisis communication to sustain vigorous interaction with stakeholders.
- Assess progress on longer-term metrics of satisfaction and trust, with special emphasis on initiatives identified through interaction with stakeholders that will benefit the organization.

Of the many assessment tools available, it is best to avoid ones that are too intrusive. Trust, on some limited occasions, might be improved through the sharing of information from focus groups or surveys, although most stakeholders will not initially (if at all) take kindly to becoming subjects of study. While it is important to gather empirical information from key stakeholders, systematic debriefing of an organization's relationship managers who are directly interfacing with stakeholders can deliver valuable information.

Different approaches to building trust will often be needed for corporate, government, or nonprofit organizations. Corporations, for example, are not generally considered to operate for the greatest good of the greatest number, but some stakeholders will not trust government for any variety of different reasons. Whatever presumptions pertain, an organization needs to find appropriate ways to talk with stakeholders and to build networks of mutual understanding and value. Remaining true to this approach will likely present challenges, failures, and some successes. However, as Prince Gautama Siddhartha, the founder of Buddhism, noted in the 5th century BC, "The only real failure in life is not to be true, to be true to the best one knows."

A powerful force working in favor of improved trust is its character as a force for community bonding. "If...trust both reduces perceived complexity and increases our tolerance for uncertainty, then conditions of increased complexity and uncertainty make trust increasingly necessary."[40] The engaging quality about trust is that people want to believe in the good of others. Stakeholders are the potential friends who will help to evolve a perception of trust for the purpose-built creation of people that is the organization.

NOTE: Revised version of a paper, "Developing the Culture of Trust in Which Large-Scale Gains Become Possible," shared at the 2010 Conference of Corporate Communication International, CUNY at Wroxton College, Wroxton, UK

References

1. The PR Coalition. (2003), *Restoring Trust in Business: Models for Action*, New York: Arthur W. Page Society
2. Goodman, M.B. (2005), "Restoring Trust in American Business: The Struggle to Change Perception," *Journal of Business Strategy*, 26(4), pp. 29-37
3. Bolton, R., R.E. Freeman, J. Harris, B. Moriarity, L. Nash, M. Wing (2009), *The Dynamics of Public Trust in Business – Emerging Opportunities for Leaders: A Call to Action to Overcome the Present Crisis of Trust in Business*, New York: Arthur W. Page Society and Business Roundtable Institute for Corporate Ethics
4. Shockley-Zalabak, P., Morreale, S., and M.Z. Hackman (2010), *Building the High-Trust Organization: Strategies for Supporting Five Key Dimensions of Trust*, San Francisco: Jossey-Bass
5. Edelman. (2009), *2009 Edelman Trust Barometer*, New York: Edelman
6. Edelman. (2010), *2010 Edelman Trust Barometer*, New York: Edelman
7. Thayer, L. (2007), *How Executives Fail: 25 Surefire Recipes for Sabotaging Your Career*, Rochester, NY: Windsor
8. Bolton
9. Jorgensen, P.E., M. Isaksson (2008), "Building Credibility in International Banking and Financial Markets: A Study of How Corporate Reputations Are Managed through Image Advertising", *Corporate Communications: An International Journal*, 13(4), pp. 365-79
10. Magee, D. (2007), *How Toyota Became #1: Leadership Lessons from the World's Greatest Car Company*, New York: Portfolio
11. Clarke, G. and L.W. Murray, (2000), "Investor Relations: Perceptions of the Annual Statement," *Corporate Communications: An International Journal*, 5(3), pp. 144-51
12. Shannon, C.E., W. Weaver (1949), *The Mathematical Theory of Communication*, Urbana, IL: University of Illinois Press
13. Allert, J.R. and S.R. Chatterjee (1997), "Corporate Communication and Trust in Leadership," *Corporate Communications: An International Journal*, 2(1), pp. 14-21
14. Tuominen, P. (1997), "Investor Relations: A Nordic School Approach," *Corporate Communications: An International Journal*, 2(1), pp. 46-55
15. Miller, Rodney G. (2009), "Sustain Funding Growth: Leadership Guide to Navigate Tough Times," Conference of the Council of Public Liberal Arts Colleges, Keene State College, Keene, NH
16. Watson, T., S. Osborne-Brown, and M. Longhurst (2002), "Issues Negotiation™ – Investing in Stakeholders," *Corporate Communications: An International Journal*, 7(1), pp. 54-61
17. Smythe, J. (1997) "The Changing Role of Internal Communication in Tomorrow's Company," *Corporate Communications: An International Journal*, 2(1), pp. 4-7
18. Johannesen, R.L. (2010), "Perspectives on ethics in persuasion", in Larson, C.U., *Persuasion: Reception and Responsibility*, Boston, MA: Wadsworth, pp. 41-69
19. Bishop, B. (2006), "Theory and Practice Converge: A Proposed Set of Corporate Communication Principles," *Corporate Communications: An International Journal*, 11(3), pp. 214-31

20. Wanguri, D.M. (2003), "Federally Regulated Corporate Communication: An Analysis of Dominant Values," *Corporate Communications: An International Journal,* 8(3), pp. 163-7

21. Freedman, J. (2009), *The Motivation Iceberg,* Freedom, CA: 6-Seconds

22. Freedman (2009)

23. Freedman (2009)

24. Phillips, D. (2006), "Relationships Are the Core Value for Organizations: A Practitioner Perspective," *Corporate Communications: An International Journal,* 11(1), pp. 34-42

25. Freedman, J. (2010), *Change Failure: April 6 Web-Workshop,* Freedom, CA: 6-Seconds

26. Goodman, M.B. (1995), "Organizational Inertia or Corporate Culture Momentum," in Cushman, D.P. and King, S.S. (Eds.), *Communicating Organizational Change: A Management Perspective,* State University of New York Press, Albany NY, pp. 95-112

27. Goodman (1995)

28. Thayer (2007)

29. 6 Seconds. (2009), *Organizational Vital Signs,* Freedom, CA: 6 Seconds

30. Elving, W.J.L. (2005), "The Role of Communication in Organizational Change," *Corporate Communications: An International Journal,* 10 (2), pp. 129-38

31. Andersen, M.A. (2010) "Creating *esprit de corps* in Times of Crisis: Employee Identification with Values in a Danish Windmill Company," *Corporate Communications: An International Journal,* 15(1), pp. 102-23

32. Galetzka, M., D. Gelders, J.P. Verckens, and E. Seydel (2008), "Transparency and Performance Communication: A Case Study of Dutch Railways," *Corporate Communications: An International Journal,* 13(4), pp. 433-47

33. McKinnon, C. and Roslyn Petelin (2010), "Complying with Plain Language Guidelines in the Corporation: If Not, Why Not?" Conference of Corporate Communication International, CUNY at Wroxton College, Wroxton, UK

34. Appelbaum, S.H., R. Lopes, L. Audet, A. Steed, M. Jacob, T. Augustinas, and D. Manolopoulos (2003), "Communication during Downsizing of a Telecommunications Company," *Corporate Communications: An International Journal,* 8(2), pp. 73-96

35. Salem, P. (2008), "The Seven Communication Reasons Organizations Do Not Change," *Corporate Communications: An International Journal,* 13(3), pp. 333-48

36. Lucero, M., A.T.T. Kwang, and A. Pang (2009), "Crisis Leadership: When Should the CEO Step Up?" *Corporate Communications: An International Journal,* 14(3), pp. 234-48

37. Horovitz, B. (2002), "Trust", *USA Today,* July 16, p. 1

38. Seglin, J.L. (2002), "Restoring Trust in Corporate America", *Time,* July 9

39. Elving, W.J.L. (2010), "Trends and Developments within Corporate Communication: an Analysis of Ten Years of *CCIJ*", *Corporate Communications: An International Journal,* 15(1), pp. 5-8

40. Miller, C.R. (2004), "Expertise and Agency: Transformations of Ethos in Human-computer Interaction," in *The Ethos of Rhetoric,* Hyde, M.J. (Ed.), Columbia: University of South Carolina Press, pp. 197-218

4: Improving Community Service

Positive behavior is much more likely to occur if it is specifically requested of people.[1]

– James Strong

What a leader does communicates best. Leaders earn credibility by achieving results. Typical challenges for a leader now are: (1) high-speed organizational change; (2) limited authority for wider responsibility; (3) adding value to the organization by helping others achieve results, at the same time as also adding value to the organization in the leader's specialization. This paper describes the application of leadership and high-speed management principles to improve the community-service-based fundraising of a nonprofit organization. An organization achieves competitive advantage in this area by delivering high-speed, pertinent community service. Let me illustrate the importance of "getting there" first, from an albeit unlikely source.

Woody Allen is credited with pointing out that the world should not be so preoccupied with invaders from outer space whose technology is hundreds of years ahead of ours. He claims it is not advanced technologies, supported by plans for world domination, that will win such a struggle. He worries about the invading force that is equipped to be anywhere fifteen minutes ahead of us. The fifteen-minute advantage would allow these invaders each morning to eat all the breakfast cereal, use all the toothpaste, and catch all the taxis in New York, or anywhere else. They would paralyze whole cities. More seriously, they could use even traditional weapons fifteen minutes before we have thought of targeting ours.[2] The same point is evident on the soccer field or in many other sports. The competitive advantage when players chase goals is the split second that decides which team's foot gets to the ball first.

For an organization to develop competitive advantage, it needs futuristic thinking in its strategic planning, to anticipate and then capitalize on future paradigm shifts.[3] For example, the popularized warnings of Alvin Toffler and others since the 1970s about the information age and the related impact on employment have translated with massive effects on people, organizations, and communities. Mega-trends in the community that might impact service organizations include projected years of peak focus in leisure and tourism, thought to be around 2020 AD and preoccupation about outer space until at least 2050 AD.[4] The valued member of an organization engineers all plans with consideration of such global trends. We need to:

- Stay close to clients/customers and competitors.
- Think constantly about new products/services and their development.
- Speed up delivery by close coordination among design through delivery or servicing systems.
- Ensure quality, easy access, and competitive pricing.
- Prepare for flexible shifts, perhaps totally out of large product or service sectors.
- Develop a culture that emphasizes change.
- Scan the globe for potential takeovers or partnerships to improve competitiveness.[5]

Important shifts of emphasis in management continue to emerge. To accommodate these shifts, this paper proposes that we now need to integrate principles of leadership[6] and high-speed management,[7] for the achievement of high performance in organizations. Leaders more than ever must focus on the global economy, visions for the future, a coach-cum-coordinator role for leaders, and access to different management tools, such as total quality management or reengineering,[8] along with principles of best practice.

Amid these often-complementary perspectives, the special value of high-speed management theory is its employment of three separate theories and sets of practices, along with its focus on "getting there" first. As Sarah King and Donald Cushman show,[9] high-speed management is especially valuable in turbulent times, which continuously require flexibility in services, systems, and people, to recognize and meet the expectations of clients/customers and the challenge of competitors. High-speed management emphasizes the speed to deliver services and to change communication processes. For this type of responsiveness, it is necessary to scan the environment, to locate operational areas where an organization's integration, coordination, and control systems can be improved; and to use a unique continuous improvement theory, to increase the speed to market of products[10] or services.

In this context, how one organization, Queensland University of Technology (QUT), set about improving its performance in community service is described here. The central community service performed through its institutional advancement unit is the focus. This unit continuously improves the delivery of community service by developing:

- Environmental scanning processes to identify the values and services its community expects to see delivered.
- Interventions for better internal cooperation, to refine communication processes that integrate, coordinate, and control the delivery of services.
- Extension of continuous improvement processes, by agreeing service standards and using detailed checklists to improve goal alignment and enhance the speed of service delivery.

Ideally, in an organization that commits to delivering high-speed community service, everyone would learn to lead the enhancement of communication. Everyone would look for ways to get closer to clients/customers and better understand the competition. At the very least, everyone is encouraged to think up better ways to get ahead of the community's expectations. Outlined below are some dynamics and pertinent background that influenced QUT's efforts to improve community service.

The Organization

QUT was reconstituted in January 1989 from its predecessor, Queensland Institute of Technology, formed in 1965. In May 1990, a major structural change followed because QUT amalgamated with another tertiary education institution of approximately similar size. The new organization became one of Australia's largest universities, with 24,000 students and 2,600 staff members. In 1993, the *Independent Monthly's Good Universities Guide* made the inaugural award of the title "Australia's University of the Year" to QUT.

Since the 1970s, QUT was a leader among Australian tertiary education institutions, with an emphasis on integrating theory and practice in its teaching programs. In addition, it supported this value by providing services to business, government, and the professions, initially by encouraging academics to provide consultancies and continuing education courses in their specialist areas of expertise. Later, it was also early among Australian universities to encourage contract research and offer enrolment to fee-paying international students. These services were part of the university's commercial activities. The total QUT budget in 1993 was $230 million, of which $30 million resulted from external funding, including research/consulting, business, fee-paying enrolment, and resource development activities.

The university strengthens its link with the community through a coordinated alumni relations and fundraising program. As in North American universities, this program secures philanthropic resources that are usually for university infrastructure. Fundraising was a relatively new activity for Australian universities, which are largely government funded. In the six years following QUT's first effort at fundraising in 1987, its total annual income was increased from less than $0.5 million in 1987 to $1.9 million in 1993 (showing a 55 percent increase on the previous year's result). This positioned QUT well to secure more substantial resources locally and internationally, for initiatives to benefit the community it serves. To sustain and to intensify these efforts, however, many more members of the university (especially leaders of academic areas) needed to see value in this focused community service. Although academic leaders understood some community needs through their own specialist lenses, few had much contact with or understanding of community leaders who had substantial influence and means.

And no one had experience directly pertinent to handling the federal government's policies to privatize tertiary education in Australia at the time. The experiences of QUT were comparable to other public sector organizations being "privatized" or "corporatized." The principles considered here may be applicable to a wide variety of third sector organizations. With mixed success, many of these organizations grapple with the challenge of deciding best practices that empower leaders and staff to strengthen relationships with the community.

Improving communication with community leaders is a central priority of successful fundraising. The process of securing, renewing, or upgrading a gift is essentially organized interpersonal communication. It is also a process by which an organization gives special meaning to what is important in the life of a donor-investor.[11] To manage person-to-organization relations, advancement staff must involve people and then track and respond to many nuances to understand and enhance engagement. A community service function grows when people in an organization develop and deploy the sophisticated leadership skills required to nurture and manage community relationships.

Typically, as an organization moves to developing community linkages, organized interpersonal (particularly face-to-face) communication increases in importance. The valued work associate, whether carrying the title of manager or not, is increasingly someone who takes responsibility for involving others in community engagement. Looking beyond routine line management of people, equipment, and budgets to develop community services as an organizational priority is not automatic and brings both opportunity and challenge. The opportunity in the budgetary climate of the 1990s was to do more with less, and the challenge was to engage work associates in processes to improve communication, consistently, day after day.

33

Communication as a Value

Enhancing communication with the community was a personal value for many at QUT. But it was the amalgamation in 1990 with another educational institution that afforded the university's leaders the opportunity to put priority on cultivating communication at all levels of the organization.[12] Communication became expressed as a core organizational value that QUT's governing board adopted as part of the university's mission and goals statement.

At that time, two perspectives about service permeated the organization. One of these was based in bureaucracy and the other was enterprise oriented. The bureaucratic outlook was truly more "inward-looking," focused on internal issues to maintain administrative processes. The operating value in this outlook seemed to be adherence to established procedures that were focused on completing sometimes burdensome processes, such as student enrolments or examination results, in time to meet official deadlines.

In contrast, the enterprise outlook was focused on creating and enhancing services to a range of clients, from students to a wider range of community members. Individuals embracing the enterprise outlook focused on creating initiatives like flexible modes of teaching, or increasing the range of "commercial" services, or outreach to community leaders and alumni. In addition to creating new services or working out how to reshape existing arrangements, this caused a rethinking of many established priorities and processes. Instead of managing cost centers or profit centers, for example, how to better meet the needs and wants of people outside the enterprise was the priority. For QUT, as for many organizations, working through the tensions between bureaucratic and enterprise outlooks was not automatic or easy.

However, federal government policy was putting pressure on tertiary education institutions to increase efficiencies through amalgamation of institutions and increasing the funding secured from the community, through payments for external services and students paying fees to reimburse some costs of the education program. The future of QUT would be largely determined by how quickly and well its academics and administrators could evolve an organization listening to its community, and how adeptly leaders developed environmental scanning to enable high responsiveness to community needs.

What the Community Expects

The idea of a university as an ivory tower of intellects opposes what the community expects from today's university. For the changed expectations of a modern university, community linkage is a measure of strength. The CEO of QUT had drawn this to the attention of the university's academics and administrators well before the amalgamation in 1990. He recognized that what the community would like is for a university to listen to it. The university that masters this skill does best.

In a community-centered organization, community leaders are invited to provide comment at every strategic move. When reviewing the mission, the marketing plan, quality system, or major programs, listening will be the first step. This requires refined environmental scanning, initially around the CEO. Learning how to listen and how to integrate listening into operations generally challenges organizations. For effective fundraising, both are daily requirements and the CEO at QUT called on the advancement unit to help spearhead the university's outreach to community leaders.

At QUT, fundraising and outreach to graduates were well-positioned as strategic efforts, grown through close collaboration among the CEO, governing board chair, foundation president, and leader of advancement. Largely because of the personal qualities of these individuals, purposeful collaboration in daily efforts embedded high-speed management principles within the framework for the integration, coordination, and control systems of fundraising and graduate engagement. It was this team that also ensured accountability to the community for the effective use of the funds secured—with advancement staff coordinating and supporting the fundraising and accountability activities. Both the QUT Foundation boards and the university's governing board provided the access to community leaders with the "wallop" required for major gifts fundraising.

The engagement of community leaders was through both individual visits and through ongoing briefings at QUT, hosted by the university's CEO and other senior management. Invitees to the briefings were selected from community leaders, donor-investors, prospects, and "hot suspects," including graduates. Briefings were mostly convened over a light breakfast, before the interruptions of a new workday, and, for the convenience of many who attended, the university's campus in the central business district was the venue. These briefings served as environmental scanning, while strengthening linkages between the university and community leaders. The briefings, as well as ongoing day-to-day interaction with community leaders, provided a wealth of information and useful follow-up opportunities for the continuous improvement of the university's community services both for its fundraising and well beyond fundraising.

The most effective mode for engaging attendees was to hold a series of two to three briefings with each successive small group. To kick off a briefing, the CEO would crisply summarize three recent achievements and changes at the university and then call on a leader of an academic program to briefly outline the main goals of an academic project or two and recent achievements. In this informal setting, the community leaders were encouraged to offer what they thought were important related issues or concerns, which they felt the university might address. In a follow-up briefing session of the same group several weeks later, a draft summary of "what we thought we heard" was presented to stimulate further comment and conversation. Importantly at this second gathering, the QUT CEO responded quite specifically to how the university might be able to address opportunities suggested by attendees and invited open discussion of the scale of resources needed to effectively pursue each opportunity. During these discussions and in later follow-up via individual visits, the QUT team listened for matches of interest and explored potential external funding opportunities to support initiatives of mutual interest.

During these efforts, it was soon clear that, for many within QUT, the least understood area of major funds solicitation was the extent of listening and involvement needed before making an "ask." From initial contact, this might require coordinated involvements of at least six to twelve face-to-face contacts, over many months or even years. The challenge of course is to shorten the time required for steps to identify a potential funder, detect a mutual interest, secure trusting involvement, and finally shape the "ask" for investment. While initially and ongoing most fundraising results were secured through the efforts of the CEO, board chair, and other members of the governing board, the involvement of academic leaders in these community leader briefings and follow-up visits also enabled some real investment opportunities. An added value of this initiative was that academic leaders experienced the quick pace with which many community leaders make decision and act. Most importantly, these outreach activities projected the organization's academic leaders as members of a "listening organization."

The interactions with community leaders helped to focus how QUT might shape initiatives to meet four main expectations, return on investment, usefulness to the community, welcoming linkages with the community, and reputation for ethical relationships.

1. *Return on investment.* Donor-investors mainly provide funds because they believe in the leadership, cause, and track-record of an organization, with a core concern being the achievement of results that benefit donor-investors. How well the university's leaders communicate this focus, with a compelling image of a desired state of affairs,[13] will be important. How well the organization delivers on this expectation is frequently determined by whether people within the organization are talking and doing something about ways to do better by donor-investors or other members of the community.

2. *Usefulness to the community.* The organization that defines its mission in terms of the benefits it brings to the community must, of course, be able to state specifically what use the community wants to make of the organization. The uses can be economic, cultural, social, professional, or

global, or all of these. Through delivery of higher quality services, a university might prove its usefulness in different ways to each of its stakeholder groups. Students will define usefulness differently to a supplier of its banking services. Leaders relentlessly ask questions to help members of the organization focus on activity that is useful to these different community stakeholders, now or in the future.

3. *Welcoming linkages with the community.* Liking others, and showing it, provides powerful entry to being liked by others. So, the organization that tells its community through a simple, visible action that it cares about and is attuned to what the community *needs* stands out. Peter Drucker illustrated this well with an anecdote about a community hospital. This hospital he suggested was, by any objective evaluation, not the most highly ranked in health-industry reviews of three competing hospitals in the region, and yet the community was full of praise for this one hospital.[14] The straightforward activity that made it so visible and valued was that two weeks after a patient was discharged, somebody from the hospital called to find out how the patient was. If a patient's report was that recovery was slow or otherwise challenged, someone from the · clinical staff at the hospital called again soon afterwards, and initiated remedial action as needed. At the end of the year, the patient also received a calendar as a memento. Although such activity was known to be routine, it said loudly that the organization remembered its patients[15] and welcomed ongoing interaction. Commitment to sustained action in this way is available to any organization.

4. *Reputation for ethical relationships.* Both inside and outside an organization, no value is more important. There are no degrees of honesty. Many religions, of course, fortunately also allow for lapses by providing for forgiveness as a basis for continuous growth. People in an organization need to understand and genuinely deliver accepted standards of courtesy, timeliness, relevance, clarity, or related performance expectations. Assurance of the fulfillment of such standards builds the trust that members of a community feel for an organization.

For competitive advantage, meeting these expectations will be evident as priorities that strengthen an enterprise culture. On occasion, members of QUT's executive-level advancement team made specific interventions to help cultivate an enterprise culture, particularly to engage leaders of the academic areas more significantly in fundraising and community outreach.

Coordinated Interventions

The first intervention was an advancement operations audit commissioned by the leader of advancement.[16] The audit crystallized serious misunderstandings about fundraising among many academic leaders. Some academics even held sincere but mistaken belief that the federal government would cut funding, or that the CEO would cut budgets proportionately with any funds raised. Such diversionary misconceptions needed to be directly addressed. Few academic leaders at QUT at the time were focused on a regular program of community outreach. Some were more experienced in fundraising than others, and each needed to be worked with differently.[17] Interventions of the CEO were needed to encourage the engagement of some leaders of academic areas.

A second intervention was that the QUT Foundation reviewed and made more explicit its own vision. QUT had set as its primary goal bringing the benefits of teaching, research, technology, and service to the community. The QUT Foundation's mission was redrafted to closely link to the delivery of this goal, by underscoring the Foundation's role to secure funds that equipped the university to better serve community needs. Any fundraising was thereby unambiguously focused on helping to develop community partnerships with academic areas, which, in turn, added value to the operations of business, government, and the professions in the community.

A third intervention commenced once the advancement staff had developed working relations between academic leaders and some community leaders who might support their academic programs. Progressively, the chair of the university's governing board, the president of the QUT Foundation, and the leader of advancement met as a group with individual leaders of major academic areas. These meetings were purposely informal, by being held in each academic leader's office area. Specific priorities and opportunities for the academic leader's fundraising were discussed. The aim in these conversations was to identify with each academic leader what were to be the agreed objectives, process, and next steps for fundraising–with a brief draft plan soon afterwards confirmed in writing.

For any specific programs within an academic leader's area of responsibility that had potential for external funding, an additional lead academic as "expert witness" was asked to draft a statement of aim, benefits, outcomes, process, and budget. The aim of each of these "project descriptions" was to clearly identify what would be the benefits from a projected initiative–for a potential funder, the university, and the community. The lead academic for a project was also asked to identify, in consultation with advancement staff, at least three CEO or board-level community leaders as potential champions or funders of the program. The goal was to establish for each academic leader a special group of community leaders able to help with the high-level community outreach required for effective fundraising.

While this proved to be a somewhat protracted exercise, the time taken to meet with and listen to each academic leader, as well as to follow through with productive actions as quickly as possible, brought some important collaborations to fruition. This intervention also helped advance the capacity of advancement staff to be credible coordinators, making use of their knowledge of donor-investors and the competitive marketplace, to successfully navigate productive partnerships with community leaders. The ongoing challenge was to inject high-speed management principles to continuously improve the number and quality of these partnerships. Some academic leaders caught the momentum and rose to the occasion, ably communicating the capabilities of the academy for the attention of pertinent leaders in the community.

The three interventions (audit, vision statement, and senior-level goal-setting meetings) were used to decide pathways for fundraising and to agree priorities going forward.

Advancement Service Standards

In addition, the advancement unit refined the process for matching the interests of academic leaders with community leaders in its quarterly review sessions. During these sessions, internal and external clients were invited to have their say on what they expected of the office. Unsurprisingly, internal clients said they most looked for "creative ideas" and "access to people with money." Although the office often met these expectations, some lead academics initially showed little understanding of the capabilities or role of advancement staff.

Following a systematic review of feedback from internal and external clients, all staff of the advancement unit met to set the quality standards for its own service. These quality standards focused on bringing added value in a timely way, to match community and academic leader interests. The standards were stated as a checklist for advancement staff to use when interacting with the leaders of academic areas:

Focus:
1. Emphasize the *benefits to others*, in terms of the difference made to the internal and external client/customer.
2. Affirm the *access* that the advancement unit provides to community leaders in decision-making positions.
3. State your *knowledge of the internal and external clients' core "business,"* by showing how stronger operations will result.

Meet or exceed expectations:
4. Agree the time to the next action and look for ways to *speed up* the offering of new services, decision-making, or closing to ask for funds.
5. Suggest actions that are *useful* to solve problems now, or to rethink services, or to reengineer processes to better meet clients/customers' needs.

6. Be *simple and clear* in all contacts, providing brief verbal or written summary as needed.

Cost competitiveness:
7. Create ideas and offer insights that visibly enhance a project's *attractiveness* to a funding source.
8. Increase income to the internal client, so the *revenue to cost ratio* improves.
9. Build *strategic teams* (by linking three community leaders to each academic leader), with expected income targets clarified.

Having agreed on these standards among the advancement staff, the advancement leader had to work with each of the advancement field staff, who would be the coordinator of the external relations efforts of the academic leaders. Taking guidance from a sales vice-president, who decided that her regional directors should run their operations independently, the advancement leader set a one-on-one meeting with each of the advancement coordinators, to clarify upcoming plans and how each wanted to interact with him. During this round of conversations, he reached explicit agreements about what kinds of decisions or problems each person would like help with, how each would update him, and how the development officers would keep each other informed.[18]

This resulted in the advancement leader adopting a tailored role as coach, which each advancement coordinator, in turn, also needed to learn, to grow into a coach-cum-coordinator role to guide the academic leaders' external relations activities. This role was not much different from what each advancement coordinator had already established with donor-investors and prospects. However, power relativities in the academy required the visible presence of the advancement leader from time to time for the interactions of advancement coordinators with academic leaders.

Checklist for "Contracted" Relations

Relationships never fit exactly with service standards. To help ensure the advancement unit's client standards were better understood from the outset, leaders of academic areas were individually invited to special all-staff planning meetings with the advancement unit. Each development officer assigned to coordinate an academic leader's external relations efforts presented a proposed plan for the year ahead, using the "Critical Step Contract Checklist" below to shape a presentation, specifying who was to do what, by when:

1. Search out QUT projects
- "Walkabout"

- Talk with leaders of academic areas
- Invite project proposals

2. Set objectives for

- Project focus to benefit community
- Access to funding sources
- Cost/timelines
- Area for development
- Making the project relevant to the community
- Assistance with writing or editing project statement

3. Identify prospects

- Match prospects and board member/QUT academics or staff
- Set strategy for briefings about projects

4. Record steps to involve prospects

- Draft correspondence for signature
- Liaise with key invitees and public affairs office for media and events

5. Ask

6. Follow up

- Draft and review agreements
- Report activities to one another and the advancement unit's database
- Obtain QUT approvals on feasibility and resourcing where needed
- Chase, receive, and acknowledge donation/investment
- Establish QUT accounts

7. Stewardship

- Arrange thank-you or acceptance event
- Liaise regularly between QUT and donor-investor
- Invoice and chase commitments
- Secure regular reports to donor-investor
- Coordinate copy for brochures and relevant publications
- Revise planning, implementation, and evaluation of what we do
- Celebrate and tell others about our success.

The proposed plans specified actions, target timelines, and person(s) responsible for each critical step, to involve individuals or groups from the community more closely and most effectively in each academic area. Each academic leader was asked to respond to an assigned development officer's presentation of the proposed community outreach plan. When agreed, commitments were confirmed in writing to frame ongoing working relationships. Emphasis was placed on using this "contract" openly between the

41

development professional and the leader of an academic area, to help build understanding of each other's expectations. This contract was also used to review expectations with the advancement leader.

The high-speed management perspective underpinning these efforts helped to strengthen an enterprise spirit.[19] To help sustain the approach as an ongoing organizational priority, individual and collaborative results were linked with the organization's professional development and reward systems. More, rather than minimal communication was encouraged in all interactions, to move toward the kind of exchange enjoyed between friends: along the lines of "treat others as we would like our friends to treat us." This collaborative approach enhanced alignments, contributing to successes.

The Way Ahead

Continuously improving the processes described above facilitated a common language and better alignment of expectations for delivering community services. Through daily efforts, advancement coordinators found they achieved most when, chameleonlike, they coordinated efforts to pull the process along. In this QUT experience, each advancement coordinator grew leadership competencies. This often required working selflessly to give glory to others for a job well done, as well as sharing in any defeat. Lao Tzu's well-known wisdom pertained, that a leader is best when people barely know of the leader's existence. It takes special qualities for people to be effective and enjoy the nuances of advancing external relations and fundraising efforts in this way.

The single piece of learning from the past twenty years about how to manage client/customer service is straightforward, namely that an employee treats clients/customers precisely the same way a manager treats the employee.[20] This realization underscores the importance for leaders of community service to advance high-speed management by example. In this context, the essential personal qualities for anyone leading community service are (1) the ability to focus, (2) organized interpersonal skills, (3) initiative-taking with competitors and clients/customers, (4) quick follow-up and response, (5) tough accountability, (6) candor about problems, (7) speedy decisions, and (8) flexibility. Largely through the development of these qualities in its people will an organization advance.

NOTE: First published as "Improving Community Service: Strategic Cooperation through Communication," in Cushman, Donald P. and Sarah S. King (Eds.) (1995), *Communicating Organizational Change: A Management Perspective*, Albany, NY: State University of New York Press, pp. 65-81

References

1. Strong, James (1993), "Chief Executive Comment," in *The Australian Way*, December, p. 4
2. Burnet, Ken (1993), "Relationship Fund Raising," Conference of the Fundraising Institute of Australia, Brisbane, Qld
3. Jones, J.W. (1993), *High-Speed Management: Time-Based Strategies for Managers and Organizations*, San Francisco: Jossey-Bass, p. 54
4. Jones, p. 66
5. Cushman, Donald P. and Sarah S. King (1993), "Visions of Order: High-Speed Management in the Private Sector of the Global Marketplace," in Kozminski, A.K. and Donald P. Cushman, *Organizational Communication and Management: A Global Perspective*, Albany, NY: State University of New York Press, pp. 71-2
6. Doyle, M. and W.A. Kraus (1982), *Senior Management Briefing: Improving Quality, Productivity, Harmony and Profitability*, TS, Author's private collection; Bennis, Warren G. and B. Nanus (1985), *Leaders: The Strategies for Taking Charge*, New York: Harper and Row; Bennis, Warren G. (1989), *On Becoming a Leader*, Reading, Mass.: Addison-Wesley; Batten, J. D. (1989), *Tough-Minded Leadership*, New York: American Management Association; Thayer, Lee (n.d.), *Making High-Performance Organizations: The Logic of Virtuosity*, TS, Author's private collection
7. Cushman and King (1993); Jones
8. Hall, G. Rosenthal and J. Wade (1993), "How to Make Reengineering Really Work," *Harvard Business Review*, November-December, pp. 119-31; Stewart, T.A. (1993), "Reengineering: The Hot New Managing Tool," *Fortune*, August 23, pp. 25-9
9. King, Sarah S. and Donald P. Cushman (1994), "High-Speed Management and Organizational Communication: Cushman King and Associates," Inter-University Center Conference on Organizational Communication, Sydney, Australia, p. 2
10. King and Cushman, pp. 2-3
11. Rosso, Henry A. (1991), *Achieving Excellence in Fund Raising: A Comprehensive Guide to Principles, Strategies, and Methods*, San Francisco: Jossey-Bass, p. 7
12. Dixon, T.C. (1990), "Reorganizing a University," *Australian Journal of Communication*, 17(3), p. 52
13. Bennis and Nanus, p. 28
14. Drucker, Peter F. (1990a), *Managing the Non-Profit Organization: Practices and Principles*, Oxford: Butterworth-Heinemann, p. 125
15. Drucker (1990a), p. 125
16. McGoldrick, W.P. and K.E. Osborne (1993), *An Audit of the Advancement Program: Queensland University of Technology*, TS, Author's private collection
17. Duck, J.D. (1993), "Managing Change: The Art of Balancing," *Harvard Business Review*, November-December, p. 112
18. Duck, p. 112
19. Cushman and King (1994), pp. 2-4
20. Kiechel, W. (1993), "How We Will Work in the Year 2000," *Fortune*, May 17, p. 35

5: Benchmarking Advancement

Tyger tyger, burning bright... [1]

– William Blake

William Blake aptly captures the single-mindedness and determination of a beautiful animal that stalks like walking grass, a part of its environment, at times indistinguishable from it, keeping focus only on what the tiger needs to live. By analogy, the tiger embodies some qualities so valuable in our colleagues, to ensure the survival and health of any organization today. As a tenacious hunter, the tiger symbolizes the obsessive follow-through and sophisticated self-directedness required of many work roles for enterprise success. Put these qualities together with a commitment to use opportunities creatively, build personal relations strategically, and take risks and we have the ingredients for the coach-cum-coordinator, who might be the only valued employee going forward–whether chief executive officer, head of division, dean of faculty, academic administrator, advancement professional, librarian, researcher, secretary, security staff member, or whomever.

Around mid-career, people might project that little more than 2,000,000 weekday minutes remain in a working life to do some useful things. The one-minute manager might glory in such a bank-balance of time. Putting aside unexpected events that could alter this projection, each day the challenge to be effective is to keep focus on what is both important and urgent. For anyone responsible for the external relations of an enterprise, which could be anyone, the priority in each day's activities should be on organized interpersonal communication and obsessive follow-through, to assure the contact with stakeholders that intentionally enhances the experience of stakeholders with the

44

enterprise. This is true wherever one works. It is increasingly true of universities seeking to be more than ivory towers.

Now and into the future, it will be the best practices that are agreed and consistently delivered that will focus the energy and humanity of colleagues to build the relationships that enable the continuous growth of the university. The development of best practices might be the greatest single challenge facing anyone who wants or needs to be working, say, five-to-ten years hence. Until the 1980's, as Tom Peters noted, everybody thought that the smallest organization was a chief executive officer with a car phone–until the first human resource placement agency emerged which outsourced presidents. Small is not necessarily beautiful. Best performance is. How we align what we do daily to advance the mission of the university in the community it serves is what counts.

Context for Best Practices

How relevant the community feels a university's mission to be is all that matters to a university's community. And the reality of relevance provides the only valid reference for refining best practices to advance an organization in the eyes of a community. This paper advocates the benchmarking of service processes against acknowledged world leaders, to enhance institutional advancement relatively quickly. Regrettably, what many (including some consultants and professional organizations) refer to as "benchmarking" is little more than "base-lining" or auditing. That approach is unlikely to be useful to organizations seeking to escape the anecdotal approaches to institutional advancement often so prevalent.

The development of best practices for a university's advancement is best commenced by first identifying why the university exists. Answering this fundamental but often skipped question is a powerful way to develop agreement among the governing board and senior management on a community connected mission for a university. Once articulated, this draft mission should be carefully explored with stakeholders, to verify whether and in what ways the university is perceived to be serving that need. Only from such realities about mission and its delivery should fundraising, grant-seeking, marketing, publications, and public relations flow.

Effective Processes

The university leaders from four countries whose insights inform this paper would not be surprised that the same principles of institutional advancement work effectively in different places, although best practices will sometimes be differently developed in different universities. A leader's knowledge of colleagues' performance, work practices, and morale provide the essential touchstones for determining the appropriate strategies and tactics to apply principles.

The framework to benchmark best practices for institutional advancement outlined in this paper is drawn from the insights of advancement leaders in Amherst College, Harvard University, Indiana-Purdue University, King's College University of London, London Business School, McGill University, Manchester University, Massachusetts Institute of Technology, Merton College (Oxford), Oxford University-Central Campaign, Queensland University of Technology, Rensselaer Polytechnic Institute, St Catherine's College (Oxford), Stanford University, and University of Strathclyde. Unsurprisingly, the leaders of institutional advancement in these universities shared similarities and differences concerning the key community need served, as well as how to meet this need.

At the time of writing, none of these world-leaders of university advancement who were interviewed had comprehensively implemented benchmarking or quality process principles. But a continuous effort to rejuvenate and refine what are broadly called best practices was everywhere evident. The paper outlines:

1) Strategic uses of organizational communication.
2) Key assumptions and practices evident in world-class university advancement operations.
3) Relevant organizational communication strategies, processes, and behaviors that might be applied in a wide range of contexts for institutional advancement.

The conclusion of the paper details a menu of concerns, from which an organization contemplating best practices in institutional advancement might tailor an approach for implementing internal or external benchmarking to develop best practices.

The steps to establish benchmarks internally or to benchmark externally against the best practices of world leaders require a thorough knowledge of one's own operation, with careful assessments of its strengths and weaknesses. As Donald Cushman noted, the steps for external benchmarking are to:

- Locate world-class leaders and competitors to benchmark against.
- Measure carefully the productivity, quality, and speed to market.
- Analyze carefully how and why the benchmark is different from yours.
- Incorporate and improve on the best practices to gain superiority.
- Continuously update benchmarking of your organization's central competitive processes.
- Remember in the final analysis, the customer is the best judge of how good you are.[2]

Given the costs and potential for failure of the benchmarking process, the investment of effort and time to address benchmarking must stay close to what gets done daily. This study of leaders of institutional advancement in fifteen

46

universities in the United States, United Kingdom, Canada, and Australia describes key concerns about where to invest effort and time, to help identify a method for evolving best practices. The observations might be adapted to other educational institutions or other organizations that have emergent or mature external relations and institutional advancement operations.

Organizational Communication for Best Practices

A leader in fundraising education in North America, Hank Rosso, told a story about that moment in airline travel when it is time to exchange business cards with the person in the adjoining seat. He indicated that when a fellow traveler noted he was a fundraising professional, he took delight in answering the "shrinking cringe" of this person with the quip, "but I'm off duty."[3] The story personalizes a general misunderstanding of the aim and character of fundraising. This narrative could legitimately stimulate a rejoinder that a true gift is given willingly, so even airline travelers should feel safe from those who are overly zealous or lack the professionalism to recognize the simple truth that a gift is to be given.

Fundraising might be better viewed as one type of organized interpersonal communication that advances an organization. Institutional advancement involves all the elements of fundraising or resource development and then takes the additional, significant steps to include planning, validation and prioritizing of needs, marketing, publications, volunteer activities, public relations, accountability—coordinated and keyed to generating understanding and support of the organization served.[4] This framework recognizes that powerful organizational communication supports these efforts through focused improvement of the understanding and support of stakeholders. What many specialists in organizational communication have known and practiced for a very long time is acknowledged in an age of rapid organizational change, that it takes effective face-to-face communication at all levels to lead organizations. Leaders in organizations listen to stakeholders to evolve strategies, or to agree adjustments to processes and behaviors. The pertinent goal always is to improve understanding through personal communication.

The importance given to listening and talking, and "walking the talk", as one management cliché puts it, was apparent in each of the leaders of institutional advancement interviewed. Whatever was a predominant personal style, it was clear that each enjoyed purposeful conversation. As one leader noted, "preaching and teaching" is the only mode that works for the advancement of the organization. Written communication is valued of course, to confirm recorded details in support of face-to-face or telephone communication.

This is just as much the case when seeking to build and sustain best practices—for which, the early personal involvement of colleagues is crucial. It is the knowledge and commitment of one's work colleagues that will most empower the efforts to target improvement. And what requires improvement will differ from one organization to another, according to its evolution as an organized operation, what values are emphasized, or the styles of leadership in play, as well as the principles that underpin its existing institutional advancement practices. The issues to be addressed will be (1) strategic, (2) process, and (3) behavioral. Identifying and implementing best practices will require attention in each of these areas.

1. Strategic Institutional Advancement

Whether in the public, private, or "third" sectors, organizations often share similar concerns about:

1. Community needs to be served.
2. What commitment to make to community needs.
3. Ways to enhance relations with the community.

Attentive leaders using best practices will ensure that the right community needs are addressed and the systems to grow leaders throughout an organization are in place. It is a truism that the right people cooperating purposefully with the right people provide the most powerful force to advance the mission of an organization. This places substantial faith in the creative power of people to do the right things. A leader's tough job is to identify, encourage, support, ask questions, but also to trust people to make the right things happen. When agreed actions enhance community relationships, the organization is positioned to grow progressively through the linkages it enjoys with the community it serves.

As a university interacts more directly and regularly with its community, a key question for a university leader is what initiatives will make a university famous in its community. Though a simple question, the answer is hard to determine ahead of time, and even harder to make happen. What will often make an organization famous is how well its people solve an important community need. In any case, the more that the institutional advancement practices encourage the university to address the substantive concerns of the community, the more aligned the university will become with more people in the community.

Focus: World and local issues deserving the attention of educational institutions abound. World population growth, health management, urban development for better living, access to the information highway, together with alienation of the information poor from the information rich, or more generally widening access to education, to name some issues that deserve the attention of community-relevant universities. When the question "why does your university exist?" was put to the leaders of university advancement at the fifteen universities studied, mutually reinforcing themes emerged. By combining the themes

48

underpinning the responses to this question, an elaborated mission for a university took shape as:

> **Educating men and women for leadership positions in the technologies, science, humanities, and the arts through a rigorous analytical approach in teaching and research, with research advancing the teaching program and, through involvement in current issues, contributing to the continued cultural and economic development of the community.**

Tailored to the specifics of a particular university, this broad statement can be used to craft a path that aligns initiatives for advancement. To do so, some consequential questions that need to be addressed are: What are the core values that will drive a university's advancement? How do we improve the understanding of a university in its community? What community needs are of such interest to the community that working partnerships between a university and community leaders are prospective?

What emerged from the interviews of advancement leaders with these questions in mind were four sets of concerns, expressed below as strategies to focus the advancement function:

Strategy 1: Concentrate each year on new major initiatives.

Strategy 2: Facilitate projects that help the university develop an international reputation.

Strategy 3: Catalyze the magic of a student and teacher seeing and using knowledge.

Strategy 4: Increase the margin of financial flexibility for university leaders.

For any benchmarking efforts to add real value, continuous innovation must edge out tendencies to standardize. The essence of the benchmarking approach advocated here is to lead change by encouraging creativity and flexibility. Naysayers will oppose approaches that seek best practices or benchmarking, just like many opposed the quality movement, because such methods are wrongly interpreted to require conformist or standardized behavior, so the argument goes, at the cost of diversity and creativity. An otherwise thoughtful leader who was interviewed, for example, suggested that benchmarking could be a "crutch." Ways must be found to overcome negative assertions about change that, when examined more closely, might sometimes be thin smokescreens for a more fundamental underlying objection that also requires careful treatment—namely, the avoidance of accountability for performance.

Strategy 1: Concentrate each year on new major initiatives

Some universities assert their significance in the life of a city or region through economic and cultural impact statements. These can be useful to frame the scale of people's energy and other resources required to address community needs. The most serious community needs will often require substantial resources to even begin to address them. Billions of dollars are spent in research to develop cures for some debilitating diseases. Multi-million dollars might be spent on urban infrastructure before any change to the lives of people is noticeable. Universities are best to focus on the community needs that are challenging but are within the bounds of reality, in terms of a capacity to serve the needs.

Given the scale required for such efforts, a university leader is best advised to navigate academic politics to help the most effective faculty secure the resources they will need. Forget the losers. A university that truly seeks high performance will get "the stars" into the productive areas and will concentrate each year on new major initiatives. An example of this approach is where one university president secured external funding for seven new buildings and 12 overseas campuses over a five-year period, by concentrating on certain key improvement areas each year. By going to foreign governments, substantial funds were also secured to teach foreign languages when the budgets of these teaching areas were under threat. Decision about what are to be the new major areas, along with regular attention to their development, requires a symbiotic relationship between a president and the lead advancement professional.

University presidents entertain widely varying understandings of what will be effective strategies and tactics for institutional advancement. It is tough for some to give the textbook "20% plus of my time" commitment to the thought and activity needed. While many lead advancement professionals would like more access to the president's time, amid the many priorities competing for that time, few experience the magic mix of a committed president, agreed priorities, mutual trust, and a regularized progression of advancement activities. Track records are built slowly in this field, but the imperative remains for commitment to long-term strategies and high-speed processes.

At one university, the president worked in partnership with city leaders to rejuvenate the inner-city blocks on which the campus was located. At another, commitment by the president and a committee to involve community leaders resulted in external funding and community access to a previously little-known art collection. Yet another conceived of most advancement activities in terms of the university's medical school/hospital, arts facilities, and technology laboratories being community resources, and leveraged funding through this positioning as a community resource. This resulted in a strong sense of community "ownership" of the university. The involvement of donors as investors was further strengthened in one case through a substantial interest-free loan from the state government, to match the substantial personal funds of community leaders, who were also given recognition for their own gifts through naming rights within the community facility.

Objectives set between the president and lead advancement professional should seek over time to move advancement from being a margin of flexibility in a dean's budget to being a percentage of the operating budget of the university. At one university that commenced purposeful resource development seven decades ago, yearly earnings from external funding, when expressed as a percentage of the operating budget, were 20%, with interest earnings from the endowment adding a further 17%. At another university that commenced resource development more recently, the achievement of 10% of the operating budget from external earnings was reason to celebrate. In this instance though, every major building constructed in the last twenty-five years contained a significant component of external funding. These achievements resulted from agreeing major new initiatives, involving key community leaders with influence and means, and long-term relationship-building.

Strategy 2: Facilitate projects that help the university develop an international reputation

The very best work in a university is distinguished as unique output to advance knowledge. In the world of ideas as in the world of action, whether of universities or individuals, reputations are built through the achievement of the difficult. Although a legitimate role of a university is also to disseminate knowledge, reputations are earned and extended through the delivery of outputs that make a difference in the world, often very directly improving people's lives.

Whether income is for the "right things" is often more important than what income is secured. Although funds for scholarships or student aid do not alleviate the yearly pressure on the faculty budget, in most universities no initiative might be more important to long-term development. University leaders in consultation with community leaders must decide strategically what are the areas for which funds should be secured, to attract the best faculty and the brightest students.

In universities that had built international reputations for research in the technologies, for example, quite substantial advancement activities focused on securing and promoting privately funded professorial positions, to attract prominent faculty as distinguished professors. In addition, each of these universities had also built privately endowed scholarship funds. The leaders of these advancement programs worked aggressively with the media, to secure featured television spots on national networks—with students explaining the outputs of projects that were completed through collaborative high school, university, and industry science education programs.

A shared concern among leading research universities was to secure funding for undergraduate research programs, thereby giving a taste for research to the closest recruitment group of future researchers, one's own undergraduates. With resources secured to attract the right students and staff for community-relevant research, substantial achievement becomes prospective. International reputations are built through focused efforts of the right students and faculty.

Strategy 3: Catalyze the magic of a student and teacher seeing and using knowledge

People give to students and students provide promise of a better future. The catalyst for a student and a teacher to see and use knowledge might be as simple as opportunity for regular face-to-face contact, or as creative as the imaginative use of one's body for dance performance, or as cerebral as the operation of equipment to probe outer space or the processes of molecular biology. Whichever the field, the value of facilities, equipment, and resources to facilitate the rational and emotional exchange between student and teacher is key.

One university used a video to show five students reflecting on their studies and what each valued about this experience. After five personal insights, the video concludes, "You have just heard five of the best reasons for supporting the endowed scholarship program." The magic that occurs when a bright student and faculty member get together, so that the student recognizes knowledge and says that she can "do it," is what advances the university. The advancement function improves understanding of this pivotal role. It is this understanding that will be a magnet for bringing the right resources to the university for faculty and students to probe the unknown. Effective communication of this function of a university creates an environment where outstanding students will want to study and do research. This is advancement.

Strategy 4: Increase the margin of financial flexibility for university leaders

It takes a good deal of time and effort to create the architecture and the processes of the institutional advancement function to impact the overall operation of a university. Moving external funding from a margin of flexibility in a dean's budget to being a major component of the operating budget of the university requires clear objectives and honest metrics, as well as time-based, achievable plans and a very strong fundraising president, who empowers with personal time and energy, as well as sufficient staff, and other resources for central advancement group. Without these, it is just an endless chain of negotiations. One long-established university with a partly decentralized fundraising function only finds this arrangement tenable because the central office controls the fundraising of the biggest component of the major campaigns.

To move the advancement program forward, direction must be agreed between the president and lead advancement professional in terms of dollar goals, specific academic objectives, a targeted flow of expendable gifts, new gifts to the university's permanent endowment, and specific capital projects—with capital development plans normally defined largely by the president, governing board, and academic leaders. To set overall annual fundraising targets, some universities target a percentage increase each year, such as a flat 20-25% increase in the first five to ten years of a new program, sliding to, say, 10% annual increase for a more established program. Such targets are often guess-work that should be informed with solid information on the size and financial depth of the donor-investor base, what level of access to community leaders is possible, and how much income is already pledged for the year ahead.

More established universities, with annual private funding of more than a hundred-million dollars might find that a 10% increase would be a serious challenge, even sometimes with the added potential of a major campaign. What is possible will depend greatly on the potential that is known about enough well-linked significant prospects. As the scale of funds raised becomes greater, flat percentage increases in income get tougher. Whatever the sophistication of the institutional advancement function, the agreement of targets needs to be informed by more than the previous year's bottom-line plus some inevitably arbitrary targeted percentage increase. Also important might be the process of extending responsibilities for raising money more evenly across senior academic leaders, so that more are actively talking with prospective donor-investors.

What the funds are used for and whether these purposes meet the goals of the university, as determined in the planning process, are important considerations for determining advancement targets. There will be dollars that the president or academic leaders would like to have, but the market will not support. These understandings should be resolved in the form of agreed financial and priority directions and objectives, which are periodically reviewed to meet changing needs. One university, with an annual philanthropic income under fifty-million dollars found a middle ground by targeting an annual 10% increase to move toward a fifty-million-dollar annual goal. When projecting income for the new year, this university knows where about 70-85% of the money might come from and hopes to raise the remaining 30-15% each year.

On the flipside, such incremental approaches can miss the opportunity to exploit potentially large gains. Rather than using such "targeting," the effective use of a true benchmarking approach requires bold moves. Ordinarily in conjunction with a comprehensive major gifts campaign, annual gains of 60-

100% or more might then be possible. Determinants for success will be factors like the influence and means of engaged community leaders, the commitment of the university's president, how well-trained and experienced are the university's fundraising professionals, the reputation and community focus of the university, the extent of linkages with a substantial number of older wealthy alumni, and the processes to involve alumni and donor-investors.

Assuming the university meets or will quickly meet such requirements, an ongoing challenge organizationally is to encourage all employees at every level to find ways to do their jobs better and to simplify core operations–this will be the basis of a university's reputation, which significantly enables fundraising success. Persistent priorities include inviting the right community leaders to participate more fully in appropriate advisory and decision-making boards of the university, along with purposeful positioning of faculty, staff, and alumni of the university on key decision-making boards in the community. Establishing and servicing these initiatives demand substantial time and cost and, while the returns might be great in the future, novices who try to match such techniques used by world-class performers may make things worse by trying too much, too soon.[5]

2. Measure Process and Achievement

Achievements in institutional advancement inevitably impact the reputation of the president and members of the governing board. Agreed reporting against goals and objectives on the performance of advancement is obviously essential. Regular meetings with the volunteer leaders who chair committees for specific fundraising programs should focus on the actions that will move a program forward. Reports in writing at least quarterly to the governing board are common, along with many ongoing informal conversations of the chair of the board and the president about achievements and progress toward achieving objectives.

Basic reporting by the leader of advancement to the president for these purposes should include pledge totals, with the most important element being dollars received and receipted. Persistently, advancement leaders advocate the importance of ensuring the president is involved in appropriate activities and that major donor-investors become friends of the president, welcomed into the president's personal life. In addition to how much is raised, the lead advancement professional will be measured "outside the box" for (1) awareness of the performance of the advancement operation, (2) whether what is raised is going to the right thing, and (3) "developmental issues," such as whether there are enough volunteer leaders being engaged to meet the current and future needs of institutional advancement.

Perspectives for evaluating the overall objectives and accomplishments of university advancement programs vary widely. One university leader identified a group of universities that he wanted to be compared with and looked at the same base year, not in gross dollars but in the percentage of income from different sources. He also watched for aberrations, such as when substantial income was secured from a single source. Another university leader noted that while he was not held accountable relative to other universities, the advancement program was held accountable for how it met the needs and expectations of internal pressures; in particular, whether there was "enough money to run the place with the flexibility needed." The key concern is that the money comes in for priorities–whether to fund the needs defined through the academic planning process or to replace money which can then be freed up for this.

One recommended practice was to look longitudinally at one's own successes; projecting back over ten years, say, to look at results such as:

- total gifts
- gifts for capital purposes
- gifts for operating purposes
- restricted gifts
- unrestricted gifts
- gifts from the basic sources, including alumni, parents, friends, corporations, foundations
- annual fund for number of donors, new donors, repeat donors, % participation, total dollars, average size of the gift, % of alumni who give.

Against these measures, growth and any aberrations in particular years were examined for the factors that contributed to the success or difficulty experienced.

Far and away, the most widely used, very basic evaluation measure was to set a revenue-to-cost objective, which has the inbuilt hazard of being too simplistic to be useful for year-to-year evaluations, much less for use as a sole measure. But, as referenced earlier, the long-term purpose of responsible resource development will conventionally be to move from, say, 80 cents net income per gross dollar in the early years to more like 90 cents net income or better, which might only be possible in a mature comprehensive program that has developed substantial major gift and bequest income streams. Comprehensive programs also set different targets for revenue-to-cost ratios for alumni, annual fund, bequest, and other programs, as distinct from major gift programs.

3. Behavioral Benchmarks

Specific, measurable objectives are needed on quality behavior that ensures revenue-to-cost results might be achieved. Quality and numerical targets to be set with advancement field staff include:

55

- active prospects and investors
- face-to-face contacts
- asks
- income per quarter.

Typically, agreement reached between a manager and individual advancement professionals on these points are specific and written. But it is the identification and engagement of right people that must drive the numbers, not the other way.

Each new quarter, agreements between a manager and advancement professionals is best recorded on a simple table summarizing realistic targets within dollar ranges, specifying what asks are likely and when. This table also records donors at program level, donors for upgrade (by date targeted), and true prospects (differentiated as new, last year donors, and past year donors). As well as details of engagement and solicitations. This information is best reviewed at least every two weeks with line management.

An appropriate pool of prospects and donor-investors is necessary for even an experienced, major gifts professional to be effective. Depending on the potential of the prospects, two to three years of effort might be needed to secure at least $1 million per year in gifts and justify the salary.

Productive Behavior

For such objectives to be accomplished, the advancement staff should focus on moving people closer to the university in priority areas, at a good pace, in good numbers. Success is achieved through activity that some organizations define as productive or chargeable hours. Productive actions are the involvements and supportive activity that bring people closer to the university. Each day, successful advancement professionals will secure appointments in the calendar to meet performance targets, prior to any other supportive or general actions. A productive goal is to exceed the needs, by doing.

In the observations that follow, some terms used that are well known within the advancement profession are:

prospect – qualified as likely to give to the university

investor – giving to the university

ask – solicitation or request for a specific dollar amount

volunteer – prominent person external to the university who assists contact with community leaders

client – anyone external and internal using the services of the university, including all listed above and university colleagues.

Actions to be considered "productive" include:

- face-to-face briefings with investors, qualified prospects, or prominent alumni

56

- other liaison with investors, prospects, or prominent alumni
- follow-up activity to satisfy the expectations of investors, prospects, or alumni
- liaison with volunteers in support of advancement efforts
- inter-office liaison for investors, prospects, or alumni, including consequent contacts with academic leaders
- writing briefing notes for participants in discussions with investors, prospects, or alumni
- planning programs to involve investors, prospects, or alumni
- research about investors, prospects, or alumni
- identifying prospects and volunteer leaders
- developing case materials, including campaign "project" materials
- proposals that follow-up with a specific ask of an investor, prospect, or alumni
- reading relevant documents/press clippings concerning investors, prospects, and volunteer leaders
- secretarial support concerned with investors, prospects, or alumni
- database entry or other record-keeping about investor or prospect contact.

All other actions, such as general administration, general liaison with internal leaders who are involved in resource development (who are called "internal champions" in some universities), publication or general brochure production, computer advice/assistance, training, and individuals' professional development, and so on, while important in various ways, should be undertaken only when five productive hours are achieved for the day. Anyone achieving better than five productive hours each day deserves a "pat on the back." Self-monitoring of achievement is crucial, but without an office system to record, reinforce, and congratulate people on their achievement, mostly this approach will remain a pious wish.

Benchmark Productive Actions

Productive advancement at its simplest is taking the right case to the right person, through the right person, at the right time, and asking for the right amount. Each of these actions implies quality choices to be truly productive. Best practice requires that the time taken for each of these steps be minimized and that the proportion of highest quality personal contacts be maximized. Just as the quality and size of a mailing list are the major influences for the success of a direct-mail request for funds, it is the number and quality of personal contacts with major gift prospects and investors that will deliver the strongest relationships and substantial investment.

Typically, regardless of the differing maturity of programs, major gift officers in the universities studied completed 12-15 visits per month, with one university's major gift officers completing 27 visits per month. This university makes a greater commitment of secretarial and administrative support staff, to make appointments and provide administrative follow-through. Interestingly, the number of asks made was consistent at 2-4 per month per major gift officer in most universities. In some larger programs, especially those engaged in major campaigns, it was common for the lead advancement professional to ask for investments as an institutional leader about three times a week. For these asks, the leader of advancement would be briefed, do the ask, and delegate follow-up actions on return. All aspects of this follow-up support for the leader of advancement were handled by an assigned major gift officer.

To sustain productive progress, a major gift officer during a year will work with 150 plus true prospects. True prospects are evaluated as having the means to give, show interest in an area of the university, and are linked through a university or volunteer leader. To secure respectable income targets, a major gift officer will intensely engage 35-50 of this prospect group at any time. From eight to twelve face-to-face contacts will be needed to secure a first major investment (from perhaps one-fifth of the prospects). Even the simplest math on this basis requires a major gift officer, ideally, to organize mutually valued face-to-face contacts at the rate of 20 per month, every calendar month.

Leading Improvement

Naysayers will dismiss this level of productivity as appropriate to someone else. A leader will acknowledge, relative to these levels of activity, whether she is "getting started, honing new skills, or staying on top" of productive action.[6] Where results are comparable to what the American Quality Foundation uses to assess profitability (that is, more than 2% return on assets) and productivity (of value added, calculated against the combined value of salary and non-salary costs per employee),[7] the advancement operation is more than novice. It is then time for an advancement leader to get on with more careful measurement of productivity, quality, and speed to deliver service. It is also the time to consider ways to involve colleagues in internal benchmarking processes.

For an advancement team still honing some new skills, one way to integrate internal benchmarking to improve operations relatively quickly is to invite the team to review the complete service cycle for the engagement of a client—from the point of view of a donor-investor, or "internal champion," or graduate, or other client. This is simply done by leading a workshop with the team to develop standards for interpersonal service that exceed the expectations of the toughest clients. Team members are asked to suggest the "moments of truth" that determine whether a client so values engagement at each key step of the service cycle to be willing to move forward to the next step on the cycle. The aim is to focus the attention of the advancement team on the communication a client needs at each step of the cycle–to be ready to move from initial engagement to further engagements, to an ask for funds or other agreed engagement, to acknowledgment, to recognition, to re-engagement for a further ask that is, larger or for a renewed gift. Each team member is asked to list thought about what a client expects at each step, such as (1) details about the organization, (2) action from advancement, or (3) access to key people. These lists are then combined, retaining the toughest expectations of clients where any overlap occurs.

To accommodate the different concerns of different client groups, separate exercises are undertaken for each group. All observations on the "moments of truth" are eventually amalgamated to a composite service cycle for engagement. When the factors that are thought to satisfy clients are agreed within the advancement team, each member of the team has a guide for deciding pertinent and timely individual actions to engage a client.

Sustaining this process requires a system for measurement that is integrated with regular performance reporting. For higher volume programs, like telephone "thank-a-thons" or solicitation for the annual fund, one organization counted the spontaneous compliments or "thank-you's" from people who were called, to calculate a measure of "client/customer delight" on a scale of one to seven.[8] Other universities use periodic donor/alumni satisfaction surveys.

To design and engage an advancement team continuously in such efforts requires focus and much energy from the leader of advancement. Some protocols that this leader might find helpful are:

1. Locate a confidante. This will also alleviate loneliness and help renew your energy.
2. Make another person responsible for tracking and measuring key improvements.
3. Integrate best practice implementation with existing reporting, rewards, and professional development.
4. Develop a template for chairing meetings to enable rotation of this role among all staff, which builds internal leadership and involvement.
5. Require a stated outcome from the start of any meeting–or adjourn.
6. Meticulously document gains, regularly refining practices to improve key measures.
7. Test client satisfaction as the only valid test.

Menu for Benchmarking: Strategic, Process, and Behavioral

Benchmarking is a commitment to catapult from continuous improvement processes to making large-scale rather than incremental gains. The determination to be the best in the world requires, "vision, trust, rewards, compassion."[9] Proven wisdom recommends focus on the following principles:

Strategically, cost-effective advancement operations sharply focus for greatest return on (1) a key community need, (2) a substantial involvement for the president, and (3) building the engagement of older alumni.

A true mission for a university will identify the community need that the university serves, a strategy to meet that need and the track record of the university in delivery. The time, energy commitment, and substantive focus of the president repeatedly emerged as the most potent factor determining fundraising success. Another leading factor was the age of the alumni. Although a university cannot choose the age of its alumni, it is important strategically to ensure that the greatest attention and resource is given to engaging older groups of alumni, whatever age these groups might be. Of course, a special focus for some universities might also be to encourage philanthropy from wealthy younger groups, where these exist, such as among the founders of successful hedge funds.

Other strategic areas to target for improvement include:

- revenue to cost ratio
- gross income growth
- unrestricted income to increase the financial flexibility of president/deans
- growth in the university's endowment for investment
- matching income to priority areas for university advancement
- time commitment to advancement by president/deans
- number of new donors (including through "donation membership" of gift clubs)
- income for student assistance (including scholarships and student aid funds)
- number of volunteer leaders recruited and involved
- marketing of priority areas for university advancement to alumni
- number of personal briefings of prominent alumni with university/student leaders
- number of alumni volunteering to assist with fundraising
- number of alumni giving
- number of events in partnership with key community groups, matched to university priorities.

Process principles are dominated by the need to shorten the time from prospect identification to ask. Most pertinent for this to be achieved are the identification and involvement of a good number of prospects and volunteer leaders, along with the development and maintenance of a good rate of asks. Implementing these principles will permit a solid base of income to be derived from recurrent gifts through 3–5-year pledges, and regular income from the three main financial sources, namely gifts from recurrent income, capital, and bequests in wills or other forms of deferred giving.

Delivery of these principles will be made more possible through:

- matching the interest of prospects to the university's priority areas
- increasing income from capital sources and from bequests in wills
- improving internal and external client satisfaction levels
- asking alumni about the value of events, recognition, and other involvements
- number of "prominent alumni" involved
- number of alumni/parents volunteering for activities (especially student recruitment)
- number of alumni/parents on university committees (hosting events, visiting alumni)
- number of university leaders on key community committees
- number of alumni sending in notes about themselves for alumni publications.

Behaviorally, an advancement team consisting of leaders will align by analogy with the capabilities William Blake's "tyger," noted earlier, as the single-minded and determinedly beautiful animal that stalks like walking grass. Volunteers, investors, and colleagues engaged in best efforts to advance a university might come to love and respect a human "tyger's" sensitive, risk-taking qualities. Persistently, a leader in this field asks president/deans, prospects, and investors **"what more can we be raising income for?"** The best institutional advancement results from consistent application of both head and heart. And the special behaviors that bring results are **initiative, energy, "smarts," follow-through, and high sensitivity** to negotiate intangible "products" with a sophisticated clientele, who have a lot of other interests competing for attention.

These tough-minded behaviors will be developed by targeting the:

- speed of follow-up
- regularity of asking president/deans what more that we can raise income for
- percentage of time spent with prospects
- percentage of time prospects and donors spend with students
- number of "moves" to get the gift
- matching the interest of prospects with university priority areas
- agreement of activity schedules to involve university and volunteer leaders
- percentage of time spent with prominent alumni
- percentage of time spent with other alumni

- number of accurate alumni records
- number of alumni accessing services, including websites and Library.

Through the development of and selection from extended lists such as these, an organization would be best to agree on eight to fifteen areas to improve at a particular time. On these, colleagues will focus.

One university, for example, agreed the following to target as leading indicators of success:

Marketing and Communications

- national and international media coverage of university priority areas
- involvement of alumni and parents in student recruitment initiatives
- interactions through website pages, with blogs and other interactive communications
- improved brand recognition/alignment among key constituency groups

Common to Development and Alumni Relations

- number of key external individuals hosting occasions to showcase the university
- number of face-to-face contacts involving university leaders with investor-prospects
- client satisfaction with the speed and relevance of university and advancement services

Development

- growth in gross income
- revenue to cost ratio
- number of new 3–5-year written pledges
- targeted income for president's and deans' priority use

Alumni Relations

- number of alumni volunteering to assist the university
- number of prominent alumni aged 40+ organized to meet university/student leaders
- percentage increase in alumni sending "keep in touch" notes for publication
- percentage of accurate alumni records.

For another organization now or for this one in five to ten years, different areas might be important. With colleagues committing to make change, the system must also be installed to measure, report on, and celebrate the achievements.

Conclusion

People like what makes a difference. The transformational leader of advancement envisions a better future, makes any self-sacrifice, has confidence in colleagues, and helps people buy into the difference each of us can make.[10] To multiply the effectiveness of advancement efforts the approach outlined can be applied across functional units, by getting these units together and requesting collective focus on the key community or client concerns to be addressed. Hierarchies within units can be demolished and people can be encouraged to build new, cross-functional teams to target key improvement areas that will deliver key results. Consistently, whether in one organizational unit or cross-functionally, the emphases for strategic, process, and client benchmarking[11] are:

Strategic

Envision what successes are possible to create long-term value for the community

- economic and cultural return on assets (requiring earnings greater than the yearly cost of assets)
- value added productivity per employee.

Process

Measure the cost, quality, and time spent on one or more of the core services necessary to achieve these for success

- service development (from identifying prospects, through case statement, to matching prospects to involvement to ask)
- securing the funds (from request/reminder to income receipt to acknowledgment to recognition)
- integrated service development (for cross-function initiatives).

Client

Improve and monitor the attributes of service that are most valued by clients, such as speed and pertinence

- Identify the service attributes that clients will value
- Assess performance
- Analyze the performance of competitors and similar organizations
- Close gaps between client expectations and the quality-of-service delivery.

Provided it is remembered throughout that the client, as defined at page 56, is the best judge of how good you are,[12] these steps to evolve best practices align the university to the community.

The benchmarking approach to develop best practices can dramatically increase the quality of services and decrease costs of operation. Only through explicit attention to critical actions, however, will desired change be sustained. It is also important to keep in mind that most leaders of institutional advancement, which potentially means all colleagues, will be comfortable with fewer rather than many leading indicators of success. As a "savvy" person in this field puts it, "Tackle what you can do today." The legitimate aim, however, is to be the best in the world rather than just slightly better than last year.[13] The best in the world welcome candid self-evaluation and encourage competition for excellence to increase the number of "tyger-like" professionals in institutional advancement.

Best practices help advance the community-relevant university, but only when we bring to the process the energy akin to that of a "tyger," which springs forward confidently to pursue what is most elusive. Delight in pursuit of the very best will ensure success. This is the basis for deciding what we should do today, every day.

NOTE: This paper collects thoughts shared for a seminar of invited senior leaders of Institutional Advancement at The Council for Advancement and Support of Education, Washington DC, May 1995.

Acknowledgment

For making this study possible, thanks go to institutional advancement leaders who participated at Amherst College, Harvard University, Indiana-Purdue University, King's College University of London, London Business School, McGill University, Manchester University, Massachusetts Institute of Technology, Merton College (Oxford), Oxford University-Central Campaign, Queensland University of Technology, Rensselaer Polytechnic Institute, St Catherine's College (Oxford), Stanford University, and University of Strathclyde

References

1. Raine, K. (1970), *William Blake*, London: Thames and Hudson, p. 62
2. Cushman, Donald P. (1995), "Continuous Improvement and International Benchmarking," Conference on Benchmarking High Performance Organizations, Oahu, Hawaii, p. 7
3. Rosso, Henry A. (1989), "Principles and Techniques of Effective Fund Raising–Fundamentals Course," Oakland, CA: The Fund Raising School, January
4. Rosso
5. Port, O., J. Cary, K. Kelley, and S. Forest (1992), "Quality," *Business Week*, November 30, pp. 66-7
6. Port, et. al., 66-7
7. Port, et. al., 66-7
8. Stewart, T. (1994), "How to Lead a Revolution," *Fortune*, November 28, p. 33
9. Stewart, p. 33
10. Stewart, p. 33
11. Cushman, p. 3
12. Cushman, p. 7
13. Cushman, p. 10

6: Beyond Benchmarking Advancement

...it's the way a thing's done that makes it right or wrong.[1]

– Augustus Saint-Gaudens

Cooperation and Common Vision

The cooperative effort of colleagues, especially organizational leadership, the volunteer board, and advancement staff, is widely accepted as the only powerful team to advance the mission of the service enterprise. Initially, this requires the board, chief executive officer (CEO), and lead advancement professional to evolve a strong working relationship. As any player of team sport knows, when a team works with a common vision and cooperation, quick follow-through is possible, thereby increasing the successes. Exceptional achievement or excellence is seen in many places: the ballet company whose principal dancer leads it to a higher plane; the sales force achieving the impossible; the rowing crew whose elegant, polished-wood shell lifts, so the water sings along the side– we can all think of poignant personal experiences that exemplify virtuosity.[2]

Following on from a benchmarking study of universities worldwide with historically successful fundraising, this paper shares insights and priorities to focus institutional advancement efforts. It outlines approaches used successfully to engage the governing board, CEO, leaders of programs, and advancement staff to increase fundraising success. It also traces the priorities and activities employed to enhance relationships with prospective donor-investors at a prominent university, along with strategies to progressively accomplish substantially more ambitious fundraising results.

Although the core advancement team in any enterprise will consist of the board, CEO, and lead advancement professional, the progressive enlistment of volunteers, externally and internally, as "champions" of resource development

65

and institutional advancement, is necessary for true success. Champions are community leaders and colleagues within the enterprise who work closely with advancement staff as advisers and facilitators of contact with prospective donor-investors. External champions have significant linkages with community leaders and specific interest in the enterprise. They might be former members of the governing board, community leaders at the board or executive level of corporations, government, or industry and nonprofit organizations, or philanthropists. Internal champions are usually at the executive level or are leaders of programs that attract strong community support or external funding. Champions are positioned to provide a powerhouse of expertise, access, or advocacy for fundraising or other areas of institutional advancement.

Enterprises developing excellent advancement practices ordinarily operate with implicit understanding of the different functions and nuances among fundraising, development, and institutional advancement. Briefly, distinctions should be drawn between "fundraising," which is producing money required by an organization, and "development," which connotes a well-organized program to include annual giving, big gift solicitation, foundation and corporation solicitation, public grants, and planned gifts, all at a more sophisticated level. "Institutional advancement" includes both these programs integrated with strategic planning that prioritizes community needs, fundraising, publications, volunteer activities and public relations—all coordinated to generate understanding and support of the enterprise. Institutional advancement becomes most productive when keyed to the strategically planned development of the enterprise.

Strategic Plan

A well-conceived strategic plan positions enterprise leaders to reach into internal and external communities, to enhance commitment to key priorities of the enterprise. Developing the strategic plan through a classic top-down and bottom-up process ensures that staff, volunteers, and any external clients feel their insights and perspectives are welcomed to help advance the potential of the enterprise.

Important operating assumptions of leadership will be to:

- Strengthen the distinctiveness of the enterprise, by communicating its "real world" outreach as a community change-agent.
- Value and respond effectively to staff and all clients.
- Build environmental scanning into activities.
- Address community change.

Confidence in the relevance of an enterprise grows when its advancement efforts enhance understandings of the mutuality of community and enterprise priorities.

The strategic plan is particularly useful for resource development to empower the collaborative efforts of enterprise and appropriate community leaders. It equips board members, the CEO, and advancement staff with the clarity to share with community leaders, coherently and credibly, the compelling priorities of an enterprise to:

- Advance initiatives for major impact.
- Build relationships for change.
- Strengthen trust in the enterprise.

Trust

A board member, senior manager, or anyone seeking to engage community leaders more closely with an enterprise is positioned to grow the mutual trust that will be needed for someone to make a substantial commitment to the enterprise. Four perceptions that enable trust to develop between people are:

- Caring and empathy.
- Competence and expertise.
- Honesty and openness.
- Dedication and commitment.[3]

Within an enterprise's advancement team, consisting of the board, CEO, and lead advancement professional, such fragile perceptions flourish when the role that each confidently accepts is well understood as a guide to collaborative action. The soundest evolution and maintenance of trust progressively develops in this team by pursuing previously agreed goals for external relations efforts that call on the varied talents and experience of the team members. Accordingly, advancement staff work closely in the shadow of the CEO to strengthen the relationships of the CEO and governing board with community leaders of influence and means.

In start-up enterprises, the founder and some immediate advisors will commit to the external relations efforts. As the enterprise grows, it often happens that the original spirit becomes lost—even in the founder, who might still sit in a reified position on the board or be an active staff person. Whether the resource development efforts of an enterprise are start-up, emergent, or mature, the priority is to keep engaging board members and other community leaders who are able, through their influence and means, to help advance strategic priorities. For these efforts, one cannot overcommunicate.

Community Necessity

An enterprise truly committed to building excellence in its external relations can readily express what difference it is making. Perhaps unsurprisingly, a basic test that community leaders frequently apply when considering whether to invest funds in an enterprise is how necessary it is—in the community's eyes. Service enterprises are not entitled to charity. And an organization that fails to deliver what the community expects will receive little support when facing funding challenges. How significantly an enterprise is serving the community's needs is a common filter for prospective donor-investors when considering whether to make a donation.

Too often the mission of an enterprise (that is, why it exists) is confused with its goals (that is, what it aims to do). A strong enterprise identifies clearly both what community needs it serves and why it does so. It is then positioned to outline the total of all the reasons why someone should support it. One agency delivering food to the homeless commences its case statement simply, "Hunger hurts." With the community need so powerfully stated, the enterprise is positioned to pursue strategies that serve this need, and to illustrate its own track record for doing so.

In this spirit, a crucial responsibility of enterprise leaders is to be able to say not only what the enterprise is doing but also what its people and programs aim to do and how it intends to keep making a difference. For example, an organization that offers a variety of services to young people might have the vision of "delivering the country's future through our youth"—a challenging and important prospect. Yet to articulate this vision, leadership needs to say what the organization must become to meet the very large needs implied in this vision.

Some enterprises take a long view of their advancement function, even designing services intended to bring return very much later. One university CEO in the 1920s, as Peter Drucker relates, set about establishing local businesses and running them for a couple of years until they broke even. Then he gave the businesses to the most promising new graduates of the university's business school, together with $10,000 in cash—a substantial sum at that time. The only request to the new entrepreneurs was expressed as follows: "You build the business and, if successful, don't repay us. Remember us."[4] Understandably, that university today enjoys a very substantial and still-growing endowment. This is true vision. Ultimate tests for any organization are how well it articulates and delivers its vision and whether its vision is shared.

In short, the case for securing investment will express how well the enterprise contributes additional value. This case will show the impact of the enterprise's resources, including finances, staff, programs, facilities, and potentially even its history. These case components that explain the authentic capacities of the enterprise should be easily accessible and translated regularly into both the public relations and fundraising programs. When the enterprise develops strategic partnerships based on this case, rather than being preoccupied with slogans and self-image, the case for resource development will be powerful—as well as being meaningful to everyone from the newest staff recruit to the longest-serving staff or board member.

Governing Board Role

To bring this case to the attention of community leaders with influence and means, it is widely acknowledged that an enterprise requires a well-networked governing board. Beyond time and expertise, effective board members provide linkages to community leaders, give at leadership levels themselves, and are also able to help identify, involve, and ask others to give. Where the board is not productively engaged with fundraising in these ways, the board chair, CEO, and advancement staff are equally responsible for initiating change. Sustaining a board's priority for fundraising remains challenging for some enterprises.

With a board too busy or reluctant to use their influence for securing funds, sometimes induction or reinduction programs for board members will be effective. Some enterprises develop systematic programs to involve the board more closely in the lifeblood of the organization, including:

- VIP tours into parts of the enterprise that are of interest.
- Presentations at board meetings by leaders of selected enterprise programs, sharing brief case studies on the aims, activities, and accomplishments of programs.

These occasions provide opportunities for question, answer, and conversation with the people delivering the services of the enterprise. This personal interchange ordinarily lifts the sights of board members and program leaders, as well as the advancement staff who facilitate the tours, visits, and presentations. The interaction can deliver new life to the board's meeting papers, with everyone involved better appreciating how to work together to share accomplishments with others.

Boards often consist of people who bring expertise, experience, or means, or some combination of these, as well as people who are on the board because they represent another group or organization, or are elected, nominated, or invited. Opinions vary considerably on what is the most desirable balance of qualities for board members, but one point is beyond dispute. For an enterprise to be effective in resource development, it is vital to build a board in which every board member is prepared to invest in the enterprise by giving and getting others to invest at substantial levels. This critical process of securing and increasing board members' investments and the engagement similarly of others must be remain an uppermost concern.

Strategic Relationships

How the CEO and advancement staff work together to build and maintain a board of such caliber endures as the single greatest challenge facing service enterprises worldwide. The time is long past for second-guessing or dancing around any shadowy assumptions about what a board member will bring to the resource development efforts of an enterprise. One powerful approach, during the process of evaluating and recruiting potential board members, is for the chair of the governing board, or sometimes the CEO, to ask each board candidate to suggest peers of influence and means, whom the board member will be able to productively engage with the enterprise. These are folks whom the board member would feel comfortable inviting to a briefing about the enterprise, which the board member and CEO would host.

Following qualification of the capabilities of each potential invitee by the leader of advancement and the CEO, an initial briefing of a board member's invitees should be set early, no later than as part of the board member's own induction and orientation. For this and subsequent briefings, the strategic plan of the enterprise serves as a filter for matters presented. Accordingly, the strategic plan should adequately reflect key programs or projects of the enterprise, address real community needs, and indicate the tangible outputs from its programs.

In addition to programmatic initiatives, the strategic plan might include infrastructure priorities, such as capital developments or even endowment to fund ongoing operations. These funds for infrastructure will sometimes be difficult to raise and require clear context for how the funds will empower the enterprise to meet community needs. Where possible, it will often be helpful to indicate how infrastructure or endowment gifts are matched by another donor or from within the budget of the enterprise.

A well conducted briefing of community leaders stimulates unplanned, productive conversations and follow-up discussions. As a community leader and an enterprise representative develop some mutual understandings in these conversations, trust tends to evolve rapidly. The "ah-hah moments" that occur in these conversations are often what catalyze real engagement. Board members ordinarily engage in fundraising more readily through these working exchanges than with the often-advocated job descriptions for board members, or planning retreats of board and staff together.

"Stretch" Targets

The chair of the governing board and the CEO also need to prioritize collaboration with the leader of resource development to reach consensus about fundraising targets. But before setting firm fundraising targets for the enterprise, it is best to discuss and reach at least preliminary understandings among the board chair, CEO, and advancement leader concerning their own giving. For a board member, CEO, or any advancement staff member to be most effective and feel most comfortable asking another to make substantial investment in an enterprise, each of these "askers" must firstly make a "stretch" investment—with a "stretch" being what others consider a generous commitment, based on what is known of the person's financial means.

Determining realistic but stretch goals for the enterprise is something of an art, but should be informed by what is known, a simple enough science! The focus should be on accomplishing realistic stretch targets, to which the board, CEO, and advancement staff can commit. For any fundraising program or campaign goal, but particularly for larger goals, such as $25 million or $250 million or greater, a most pressing question to answer is who the lead prospects (not suspects) are. That is, true prospects who are linked to the enterprise, with each qualified as able to give better than 10% of the overall targeted goal. Four to five prospects, not one, per investment at the upper level of a gift-range chart will be needed.

A sobering exercise when anyone plucks fundraising goals from the air is to ask such "target-setters" to put real names of prospects at each of the investment-levels needed on the gift range chart. The cold realization of the effects of a failed fundraising effort usually dawns, especially where it is a public campaign. Conversation of this kind also provides an opportunity to recommend the closer involvement of more people who have the influence and means to help.

Community Leader Relations

Many people with capacity to make substantial gifts are tired of being asked to give to organizations unable or unwilling to illustrate how their gifts make a difference. A powerful advancement team will view external funding from the point of view of the funder, as investments that extend the delivery of benefits to the community. And the advancement team will keep in touch with a donor-investor about progress for the delivery of results from each gift. Persistently improving this process has seen the annual fundraising of some organizations double or better in less than five years, while also dramatically increasing the number of donor-investors.

Any externally funded initiatives, whether community-based support programs, clinical services, a professorial chair, scholarships, applied research, or another initiative must make an appreciable difference for the community within a specified timeframe. Each agreement to fund such initiatives implies a contract of care, with the terms of funding agreed with a donor-investor to implement an initiative clearly understood. Confirmation is to be in writing, via a confirming

71

proposal, letter of agreement, or memorandum of understanding that also indicates reporting and accountability measures. This may include inviting a donor-investor to have some level of involvement with the progress of an initiative, up to the extent permitted by law.

For substantial programs or any that fund personnel appointments, a strategic advisory group may be established at arms-length from the donor-investor, to monitor performance against expectations. This group will consider and agree milestones developed with the pertinent program leader, who will have line responsibility for performance. Throughout the term of a funded initiative, regular information exchanges are to be sustained to keep the donor-investor apprised of the progress of the initiative.

Continuous Improvement

In partnership with the CEO, the advancement office is charged to assure the quality of interaction with donors and the wider community. This understanding is continuously needed to do better what is already being done well. While enthusiasm for quality processes has waned on some lecture circuits, many organizations in the private and public sectors rightly continue to encourage coordinated quality assurance. Enterprises that have lightly integrated processes for assuring quality outputs are reaping continued benefit.

Most critically, the CEO and advancement leader need an informed understanding of the quality and number of relationships with influential donor-investors. Key records needed for this include not only global summaries but also the means to drill down to various levels of detail about interpersonal contacts, including solicitations, written proposals submitted, and reports on the use of funds. Although the main reason for failed fundraising efforts is that not enough "asks" are made, the equally important and related reason is that there are insufficient prospects at the levels of giving needed to assure success. Only by involving enough people of sufficient means in the enterprise are major comprehensive fundraising efforts likely to succeed.

Although the program leaders who benefit from external funding are the line managers responsible for delivering results, the advancement office assures accountability to donor-investors. Sometimes, this may require the CEO to lean-in to ensure program leaders make timely and effective use of funds, which is fundamental for sustaining the trust that donor-investors put in an enterprise.

Relationship Value

Levels of trust are most strengthened with donor-investors or other external clients through the delivery of promised results. Trust is the core value for growing all relationships and is the strongest force for the continuous improvement of efforts. Helpful to engendering trust also is to ask donor-investors, leaders of programs, and other clients what more the enterprise could be doing, and how the services might be improved.

In the early stage of fundraising efforts at one university, a survey of internal clients found that the purpose of fundraising was not well accepted. In response, the advancement staff commenced a program to illustrate their purpose and how to work collaboratively to secure major gifts. Some of the initiatives that proved useful in this case were:

- Senior managers of program areas participated in sessions about effective fundraising (facilitated by an external fundraising specialist).
- Advancement liaison officers were assigned to program areas with the highest fundraising potential to agree collaborative efforts.
- Focus groups were held with internal clients on advancement opportunities.
- Advancement staff periodically participated in the executive meetings of academic areas, and, in turn, leaders of academic areas periodically participated in the staff meetings of the advancement office.

At this university too, the leader of advancement requested an independent audit of the advancement operations, by two experienced vice-presidents of institutional advancement. This resulted in suggestions to refine the advancement processes, including specific ways for senior academic leaders to be more productively engaged in fundraising.

Subsequently, a survey of internal and external clients, who had continuously worked with the advancement office in the preceding year, was conducted to determine expectations and satisfaction levels. Forty-five major donors and fifty-one academic leaders responded to the survey, with 84% of responses rating performance at the excellent or good levels. As a result of specific suggestions in these responses, leaders of academic programs and their liaison officers from the advancement office adjusted some aims, expectations, and processes to enhance ongoing efforts. This kind of self-evaluation helps everyone along the path to building excellence.

To broaden involvements in fundraising beyond the governing board and senior leaders, this university also purposefully engaged the leaders of academic programs in a five-year major gifts campaign. In addition to securing the university's largest donation at that time, of $2 million, the face-to-face briefings that the academic leaders hosted for investor-prospects were greatly increased. This enabled the more broadly based "horsepower" of some academic leaders to get to know additional community leaders, including from among their own alumni.

It is reasonable to expect that as this formative advancement office continues to evolve, income results will continue to grow, with the cost to income ratio of fundraising commensurately dropping as funding grows. Over a five-year timespan, even with operating costs modestly increasing, expenditures might remain well below 20 cents to attract each gift dollar. This compares with 25 cents in costs per gift dollar, cited as a standard by pertinent professional bodies for an organization at a similar stage of evolution.

Benchmarking

Ongoing improvements to the advancement operations of the kind outlined above are pre-requisite to seeking even more substantial gains through systematic benchmarking. Much can be learned through internal benchmarking, particularly to increase the rigor of goal-based actions. But much more can be accomplished by benchmarking against world leaders.

The benefits then include access to details about exceptionally successful processes and new ways to advance the productivity of board members, enterprise leaders, and advancement professionals.[5] Establishing meaningful benchmarking, however, is demanding on energies and time. The enterprise that rushes in without enough preparation can flounder, and one that does not move quickly enough can lose momentum.

Internal Benchmarks

Internal benchmarks typical of what might be used to develop specific targets are outlined below, using generic "enterprise" terminology:

1. Common to fundraising and external relations
   - External champions hosting briefings with peers to showcase the priorities of the enterprise.
   - Face-to-face interaction of champions with donors and prospects (briefing visits to donor-investors; awarding of honors or recognition at professional conferences, outstanding service recognition, gatherings to updates former board members, regular CEO breakfasts to brief community).
   - Client satisfaction with the speed and pertinence of services.

2. Fundraising
   - 10-20% annual growth in gross income.
   - Cut the cost to revenue ratio (by an agreed percent of costs for each dollar raised).

- New three- to five-year written pledges at major investment levels.

3. External Relations
   - Engage well-placed champions to assist the enterprise in specific leadership roles.
   - Invite prominent community leaders to meet with enterprise leaders; and, in the case of a university or college might include:
     - o 100% increase of alumni or other "clients" sending information to be published in keep-in-touch notes.
     - o Increased number of accurate alumni/client records.

The targeted expectations agreed between an advancement leader and staff for internal benchmarking emphasize raising sights, to seek substantial rather than incremental growth.

Process Documentation

At the university mentioned earlier, to monitor and keep improving the processes to strengthen satisfaction levels among internal and external clients, the advancement office additionally completed ISO9000 quality certification. This was done by the advancement team documenting quality processes. The advancement team's own sense of commitment was enhanced using this well-tested approach for improving service delivery. The documented quality processes of the advancement office were independently approved for the quality certification.

Accordingly, as the internal benchmarking got underway, each core advancement process already had a documented guideline for actions. The framework used to document quality processes was the cycle of steps commonly used to find and engage prospects, along the lines broadly outlined below:

1. *Initiative identification.* When a resource development initiative is identified as a priority area, in consultation with a program leader, the advancement staff member responsible for liaison works with the leader of a program to prepare an outline for fundraising—stating aim, benefits, outcomes, process, and budget for a "project."

2. *Prospect identification research.* An advancement officer will continuously contribute to prospect identification, by drawing on the knowledge and contacts of external champions in the first instance. Prospect identification research is conducted through:
   - Peer-level contact with external champions, including peers of governing board members and the CEO of the enterprise.
   - Public records and information services, newspapers, magazines, databases, reference sources, and market research

services, to uncover details of the wealth and interest areas of potential prospects.

- Internal contacts, that is, an internal champion may already know of an organization or individual with specific funding interests.

Once a prospect is approved by the advancement leader (or designee), a development officer arranges conversations (predominantly face-to-face) between the prospect, a pertinent advancement staff member, and nominated champion(s).

3. *Ask.* Within three months, a development officer is responsible for strategizing and setting the timing for an ask. The development officer comprehensively briefs the person who will make the ask. This will normally be an enterprise or community leader who has the strongest linkage and best fit of interests and personal style with the prospect. All contact is recorded immediately after any interaction on a file note, directly in the computerized database and hard-copy files.

4. *Acknowledgment.* When an ask is successful and the level of gift is agreed with the prospect, a development officer provides to the leader of advancement the proposed terms of the gift in writing, which are to be signed-off by the donor prior to signature by the appropriate enterprise leader.

5. *Recognition.* Appropriate personalized recognition is to be set according to the amount and nature of the gift. If, for example, the gift is at a level designated as strategically important to the growth of further philanthropy by the donor or others, or is otherwise strategically significant to the enterprise, the donor should be formally and individually recognized at an appropriate event, with recognition to include an appropriate certificate, plaque, or memento that will be meaningful for the donor. All donors are to be acknowledged with an appropriate personalized thank-you letter within 24 hours, followed by further personal face-to-face thanks individually or in group events appropriate to the level of giving.

Transition to External Benchmarking

When consistent gains are recorded against internal benchmarks for at least several quarters, benchmarking against world leaders may be considered. Potential readiness for this step is indicated by a continuously improving level of performance across the core areas targeted for the internal benchmarking. Especially important when deciding whether to undertake external benchmarking is the overall confidence that both the CEO and leader of advancement feel for the maturity of the advancement office's system of engaging and stewarding donor-investors.

External benchmarking will require agreement with one or two world leaders, who are willing to participate for two or more years in the ongoing measurement and follow-up conversations and conferences about optimal processes—which is much more intensive than simply comparing data. Accordingly, the advancement office in this university sought out two international universities (McGill University in Canada and Strathclyde University in Scotland) and shaped a carefully outlined set of understandings for the benchmarking. In this case, the benchmarking partners agreed to enhance the speed and effectiveness of engaging major gift prospects as donor-investors. Each partner focused on sharing ways for involving key prospects.

An immediate benefit from the partnership was that the interest of the university's CEO was piqued to improve how industry-funded professorial chairs were managed. A new procedure that was developed was modeled on the approach of one of the benchmark partners. The buy-in to implement this procedure helped to close the previously substantial time-lag from when the industry source agreed to fund a professorial chair and the date on which the appointment was taken up at the university.

Priorities for Achievement Beyond Benchmarking

This university had built notable successes during little more than a decade, including:

(1) Two comprehensive campaigns that achieved results beyond goals.

(2) Continuous improvement of fundraising processes that worked well, and

(3) Initial phases of internal and external benchmarking completed.

With these successes in hand, the university was positioned to consider the next level of ambitions for the university's fundraising, through a third comprehensive fundraising campaign. This would require the systematic engagement of community leaders with university leaders, at even more ambitious rates. To commence this "advancement beyond benchmarking," the university projected a five-year development plan.

Five-year Targets. Targets were set initially to build relationships with a much larger number of prominent alumni and community leaders who had potential to support priority areas of the university, along with consequent increases in targets for funding and engagement. The increased efforts were to seek:

1. Partnerships with 200 leading organizations and a further 500 prominent individuals.

2. Annual fundraising income of $5 million and a substantial endowed investment fund.

3. Personal involvement of all graduating students and 10% of total alumni.

For these targets to be realized, it was necessary to have board members, internal/external champions, and advancement staff in place who liked bringing community leaders to campus to experience the university's people and programs. The development field officers were seasoned professionals, able to keep actions timely and pertinent. They were well-experienced working with board members and to agreeing clear expectations and understandings with prospective donor-investors. Internally, through the university's planning process and during regular contact with the academic leaders of program areas, the advancement officers were continuously identifying strategic initiatives of potential interest to prospective donor-investors.

The leader of advancement oversaw the quality of all briefings, visits, and ongoing fundraising, reporting every two weeks to the CEO on progress. The advancement office met weekly to review progress against priorities, with particular attention to progress on key initiatives. The office also periodically held problem-solving sessions to consider new activities or to modify operations. Surveys of the advancement office clients were conducted at least annually, and advancement staff continued to improve advancement processes through their self-critical performance reviews with the leader of advancement.

While strengthening its position within traditional, local, and regional constituencies, the university additionally expanded its range of relationships with nationally and internationally based corporations, foundations, alumni, and non-alumni individuals. Somewhat belatedly, it developed and shared information about ways to make financial commitments through bequests in wills and other planned gifts.

Integrating Enterprise and Campaign Vision

Because the university had enjoyed progressive success with a variety of advancement initiatives, it was felt that tackling the more ambitious goals for a substantial, comprehensive campaign would transform advancement efforts further. The strategy was to bring the fundraising and external relations efforts to the levels of quality and effectiveness characteristic of the best programs.

Preparation for this campaign would require intensified and wide engagement of leading clients, such as alumni, as well as the increased involvement of corporate, foundation, and other community leaders. At the heart of campaigns are relationships, especially stronger relationships with people who can make leadership gifts to advance strategic efforts (of at least $100,000 and greater). For people to make gifts at these levels, an enterprise must become an emotionally significant part of the life of each prospective lead donor-investor.

The following framework describes the integrated efforts that this university used in its planning the major campaign to build on its successes. The CEO, leader of advancement, and three development field officers, committed to six months of initial preparations that were focused on progressively engaging enterprise and volunteer leaders at higher rates. The CEO and advancement leader liaised closely to agree the shape of the campaign and to review progress on each of the priorities below.

1. Refresh Identified Needs

Prior to launching a major fundraising effort, it is important to revisit and reevaluate alignments of the enterprise with the perspectives of community leaders. It is important to understand early what programs or future initiatives might have most potential to attract funding.

Assessing what prospective donor-investors view as the most pressing community needs is best done by reaching out to a wide swath of influential and affluent community leaders, including well-positioned alumni or other clients. To assemble information for this assessment, gatherings were hosted by the CEO and/or board members with the support of advancement staff at locations where the concentrations of wealthy investors and friends were greatest. These gatherings also served as early cultivation of prospective donor-investors, using a format that encouraged conversations about:

- What issues are expected to confront the range of clients served by the enterprise, up to, say, 25 years hence.
- What understandings and skills people need to access the enterprise.
- How the enterprise can make a difference to the daily lives of people.

Ideas, comments, and themes from these consultations, help clarify points to underpin the longer-term strategic advancement of the enterprise, which in turn will shape the campaign plan.

Targets

- Identify at least sixty prospective lead donors, of whom a maximum of ten are already involved in the enterprise (that is, ten among sixty potential key volunteer leaders).
- Draft an advancement strategy to address pertinent community needs, to help determine the enterprise's future needs and priorities, for the consideration of the CEO and the board.

2. Prepare a Written Campaign Plan

The campaign plan presents the case for supporting the enterprise. In the drafting of this plan, it may be possible and helpful to incorporate pertinent "nuggets" of detail that community leaders have shared in individual conversations or group gatherings, to align the campaign plan most closely with these interests. The campaign plan highlights how staff and volunteers are to emphasize the added value of activities at the enterprise. For example, a college or university might emphasize:

- *The magic that occurs when a bright student and staff member work together to pursue excellence*–in doing so, each adds value by exploring new ideas to put knowledge to work. When translated into a case for support, cameo stories on this theme will celebrate the variety of how students make use of what they learn in the classroom or laboratory, through internships, performance, or cooperative education, as well as in community projects or competitions in which they participate successfully. What most powerfully showcases students at an educational institution will be the students' personal growth. People are often most interested in giving to students–believing that students provide the promise of a better future.

- *The accomplishments of graduates who add value to the community*–for example, graduates who have built well-rounded, successful lives while striving for excellence. These folks add value locally, nationally, or internationally in areas such as the arts, sciences, business, the professions, or through public service.

- *New major initiatives and plans of the board, donors, or staff* that add value to the services offered. The purpose should be to strengthen how everyone can contribute to the development of the enterprise.

Target

- Draft campaign plan presented as an appendix to the strategic plan of the enterprise.

3. Intensify Donor Research and Evaluation

Identify at least 300 individuals or organizations who have the ability, with appropriate involvement, to make leadership gifts, from $100,000 up to preferably 10% of the campaign goal:

- Set face-to-face group sessions with members of the governing board, champions, or other community leaders, who are likely to have extensive personal or professional networks. Systematically seek their assistance to identify wealthy individuals with potential interest in the enterprise.

- Establish "desk research," using Internet search engines and research services, such as investment services, to profile the wealth, philanthropy, interests, and linkages of prospective lead donor-investors.

Target

- Ensure at least five detailed and five brief profiles of prospective lead donor-investors are completed per week–to be sustained continuously beyond the initial campaign planning stage.
- Establish scanning of news reports and public stock/financial information on lead prospects, for weekly summaries.

4. Increase the Number of Face-to-Face Communications with Wealthy Individuals

Grow the number of individual and team visits to lead and prospective major gift donors, enhancing the stewardship of gifts, matching interests to priorities in the strategic plan. As appropriate, ask for initial gifts, or renew and upgrade levels of giving.

Target

- Average four visits with campaign prospects each week by leading enterprise representatives (CEO, leader of advancement, other professional staff, or volunteers).

5. Review Processes of Annual Fund

- Analyze year-to-date results of giving within segments of donors for all levels of giving, evaluating communication practices used.
- Find opportunities to engage more closely the donors who are making lead gifts to the annual fund, by building connections with people in the enterprise, matched to the specific interest(s) of donors; improve telephone caller training; and strengthen the emotional impact of communications and mailing packets, adjusting as needed.

Targets

- Adjust annual fund to achieve results targeted for the current fiscal year.
- Agree on processes to achieve increased targets, to be targeted for the next fiscal year.

6. Personalize Communications

Review advancement invitations, correspondence, phone protocol, publications, and website pages. Wherever possible, be more personal and interactive:

- Coordinate telephone "thank-a-thons" and conversations about the enterprise with all current donors, in preparation for solicitation in the next fiscal year.
- Coordinate handwritten notes or personal emails to any donors not reached by phone, for thanks and subsequent solicitation.
- Personalize communications between leaders of programs and donors to the programs funded.
- Identify and engage donors or friends with potential to be advocates for the enterprise. Initially identify one to two potential advocates in at least ten areas of the enterprise that are strategically important for funding.
- Tailor acknowledgment letters to donors of larger gifts.
- Ensure for all gifts that receipts and acknowledgments are mailed within 24 hours of gifts being received.
- Establish informal "mixers" and other opportunities for regular interaction between donor-investors and the leaders of programs.
- Engage donor-investors as appropriate in planning and implementing regular telephone calling to other donor-investors to invite attendance at selected enterprise events.
- Conduct surveys of the satisfaction of internal/external clients with the services of the enterprise, in collaboration with public relations staff.

Targets

- Reach at least 1,000 prospects and donor-investors for a telephone "chat"–for thanks or "catch-up," not for fundraising!
- Complete personal notes to all others.
- Coordinate progress reports from all program leaders to donors who support them.
- Engage at least ten to twenty people as advocates of the enterprise within potential funding organizations, such as foundations and corporations, and confirm a program for continued interaction.
- Ensure donor acknowledgment standards are met.
- Hold at least two informal "mixers" with major donor-investors, board members, and the enterprise CEO each year.
- Pilot telephone outreach from donor-investors to fellow donors, initially to invite support through attendance at events.

- Establish baselines for evaluating the levels of satisfaction with the communications of the enterprise across a wide range of people in the community.
- Complete any outstanding projects targeted to improve communications.

7. Increase Recognition of Accomplishment

Beyond giving public recognition for the accomplishments of people linked to the enterprise in its publications, personalized communications are even more valuable. The advancement office should prepare congratulatory notes for the CEO to send to anyone linked in any way to the enterprise who receives community or professional honors or awards. Where possible, similar notes should be arranged from program leaders or professionals in the enterprise who have dealt with the person.

The range of opportunities for an enterprise to recognize people more personally include:

- Arranging recognition of accomplishments at conferences and in public or professional meetings.
- Distinguished achiever awards.
- Leadership seminars where specialist expertise is recognized and shared by inviting an individual presentation or by participation on panels for community, professional, or enterprise workshops.
- Seeking input on planning and marketing task groups or for the further development of community involvement with programs of the enterprise.

Targets

- Identify further opportunities to highlight accomplishments at scheduled events.
- Present an award that recognizes significant community accomplishments, ideally monthly, with at least two awards each year that recognize distinguished volunteer service in programs of the enterprise.
- Invite community leaders to share their specialist perceptions and expertise in seminars for staff, clients, or the public. Progressively seek to expand this initiative to two seminars per month.
- Each major program area should suggest opportunities for community leaders to similarly offer these seminars, as possible, for community or professional groups affiliated with a program leader.

- Recruit "champions" from the "friends," or any similar associations or groups affiliated with the enterprise, to recommend marketing opportunities for increasing community attention for public events of the enterprise.

8. Review of Records and Database Support

Assess the accuracy and responsiveness of the advancement unit's record-keeping, including database entry, checking, and reporting processes. Review the capacity of the information system to be used for increased networking, including intensive relationship marketing.

Target

- Agree on best practices for records and database entry and the scheduling of reports.

The specific targets agreed for any of these areas must be appropriate to the capabilities of the people and resource constraints that will enable success to build on success. Deciding which of these areas are to be tackled, along with what targets are to be agreed, must be arrived at carefully to sustain a workable approach.

Internal Communication Program

A well-considered internal communication program will thank internal donors, champions, and colleagues who support resource development initiatives. Informal "mixers" of non-advancement and advancement staff, when held regularly, are one way to encourage greater understanding of how advancement staff and others within the enterprise might work together.

Additionally, it can be productive to periodically ask each advancement staff member to find an excuse to telephone two non-advancement staff members for a chat about how someone recently worked successfully with the advancement office. Setting brief reports on these conversations at advancement staff meetings can make this exercise more than a pious wish of the advancement leader. Print media and websites of the enterprise should also be regularly used to illustrate the success of colleagues who secure funding by working with advancement staff.

Conclusion

Where better than three-quarters of the targets for priorities 1-8 listed above are accomplished, the enterprise has evolved a system for achieving excellence in institutional advancement. Where better than two-thirds of the conditions are in place, the enterprise has some capacity for excellence but has much to do. Anything less than this and the best course in considering whether to launch a major campaign, is to wait and work.

The result of failed comprehensive campaigns can be as much as five years of cynicism and major future blockages to effective relationships among colleagues, clients, and donors, which might even lead to challenges for the survival of some enterprises. In addition to achieving dollar goals, the benefits of excellent resource development include a greater involvement of community leaders, an increased capacity to truly meet community needs, and the advancement of the long-term development of the enterprise.

NOTE: First published as "Beyond Benchmarking Institutional Advancement: Jump-start to Fund-raising Excellence," in Cushman, Donald P. and Sarah S. King (Eds.) (2001), *Excellence in Communicating Organizational Strategy*, Albany, NY: State University of New York Press, pp. 139-62

References

1. Saint-Gaudens, A., (2009), *Augustus Saint-Gaudens: Master of American Sculpture.* December 28 Television Broadcast on KTEH
2. Thayer, Lee (n.d.), *Making High-Performance Organizations: The Logic of Virtuosity*, TS, Author's private collection
3. Sheldon, K. (1996), "Credibility is Risky Business: An Interview with Vincent T. Covell, *Communication World*, April, pp. 16-9
4. Drucker, Peter F. (1990a), *Managing the Non-Profit Organization: Practices and Principles*, Oxford: Butterworth-Heinemann, p. 125
5. Carbone, Robert F. (1989), *Fundraising as a Profession*, Clearinghouse for Research on Fundraising, College Park: University of Maryland; Worth, Michael J. and James W. Asp III (1994), *The Development Officer in Higher Education: Toward an Understanding of the Role*, Clearinghouse on Higher Education, Washington DC: George Washington University

7: Sustaining Funding Growth

---

for the best and worst of times

It is important to understand how economic turmoil impacts a nonprofit organization's fundraising, and why, for some organizations, this makes for the best of times and for others the worst of times–along with what actions organizational leaders take to seek the best of times, despite the economic challenge. The focus of this paper is how organizations sustain and grow fundraising in tough economic times. The purpose is to help gather and organize a coherent approach to planning and executing a sustainable fundraising program for such times.

By drawing on the experiences of the leaders of organizations and institutional advancement, as well as board members and consultants, the paper proposes a 3-Step approach to developing best practices for sustaining fundraising–an approach that is also applicable in the best of times. The conclusions and recommendations here are synthesized from inquiries, consultations, and observations of best practices in universities and colleges in the United States, Canada, United Kingdom, Australia, and New Zealand, during the tough economic times of 1987, 1990-91, 2001 and the 2008 meltdown.

NEWS FLASHES:

"…where donations to universities are still a relatively new concept…The University of Auckland, New Zealand's largest, launched the campaign with the announcement it had already raised $48 million from a range of significant donors…" **November 23, 2008** (universityworldnews.com)[1]

"Despite beginning and ending during serious economic recessions, the most ambitious fundraising campaign in state history soared past its $600 million goal to raise $853 million..." **January 30, 2009** (pmr.uoregon.edu)[2]

"Indiana University and its fundraising partner, the IU Foundation, today announced that they are raising the goal by $100 million, or 10 percent, to $1.1 billion...campaign, which runs through 2010, already has realized 95 percent of its initial $1 billion goal..." **February 6, 2009** (iufoundation.iu.edu)[3]

"Over half of companies increase their philanthropy in 2008, despite economic decline." **June 2, 2009** (corporatephilanthropy.org)[4]

During the economic meltdown of 2008, these good news items amid the repetitive gloom of most news media might have heartened some but were viewed by others as being against the overall trend.

In mid-October 2008, the president of one regional, tertiary education institution reported to colleagues that a donor had visited to write a check for half-a-million dollars, as well as to affirm the next three annual payments of the same amount. At another organization providing after-school educational programs nationwide, donors were in touch to establish, renew, or upgrade giving. Consider too, that in June 2009 when I asked chancellors, presidents, and other senior leaders of state liberal arts colleges at the beginning of a workshop to share any good fundraising news, the responses were:

- $3 million gift, plus matching funds
- higher alumni giving
- annual fund increased, and
- three organizations reported increased philanthropy for financial aid for students.

The following week, during a telephone call with a consultant, mention of these good news items from the workshop stimulated his observation that even a soup kitchen (his client in a major city, and to many a classic indicator of the state of the economy) had experienced a record increase in funds raised through direct mail. During the phone call, we speculated these organizations must have made a substantial investment in organized fundraising programs over many years. But a closer look revealed that almost half were modest fundraising programs, better described as "start-up," "formative," or "pre-emergent."

Additionally, the educational organizations surveyed for the Target Analytics of Higher Education Fundraising Performance for 2008 reported that the number of donors declined but total giving was up.[5] This report observed that, although the donors who were giving tended to give more, they were also becoming more selective about the charities they supported. Private educational institutions were seeing a modest decrease in median revenue per donor, and public schools had a modest increase. These reported results aligned with personal observations, particularly early in 2008 at the onset of the downturn.

Sustaining Fundraising Success

The most successful organizations put increased emphasis on soliciting gifts from trustees, other lead individuals, private foundations, and planned gift prospects. Education-related organizations that sustained or expanded income did so by focusing fundraising in areas of perceived high value, such as for STEAM (Science Technology Engineering Arts and Math Education), or for research to improve the diagnosis and treatment of medical conditions that impact substantial population groups. As in less-straining economic times, fundraising success required crisp focus to communicate the real value of the exceptional services that an organization delivered to people.

Early in 2009, a survey of institutional advancement leaders[6] that probed how each was addressing the economic challenges distilled that:

1. Impacts on the direct marketing efforts of nonprofits seemed to lag the economy, and the effects on giving did not necessarily parallel other financial declines, such as consumer spending.
2. Organizations with community-relevant missions showed the most potential to sustain higher levels of giving.
3. Shifts of effort toward soliciting larger gifts, especially from trustees, other lead individuals (including past donors for both current needs and planned giving) and private foundations, helped to offset declines in some other areas, such as the annual fund.
4. Organizational leaders with access to or engaged with well-networked philanthropists were most able to reach out to secure new larger gifts.
5. Organizations that fared best had leaders whose approach to fundraising was continuously in a mode of sequencing or concurrently conducting campaigns. These leaders were diligent about communicating expectations, partnered with the advancement team, used creative problem-solving, were flexible, made a hands-on commitment to personal visits with prospects, and followed-up personally on substantial gift opportunities.
6. Some formative and emergent fundraising programs, in which a few new major gifts had a relatively large impact, fared better than some mature programs. Mature programs with mega-campaigns were significantly impacted by some lead donors suffering such substantial financial losses they were unable to honor campaign pledges, causing several well-known mega-campaigns to lower campaign targets.

For some organizations, extreme anxiety about the economy induced a "sit-on-the-hands" approach. In these cases, even soundly rational reminders that the biggest reason for prospects not giving was that they are not asked could not induce leaders in these organizations to overcome inhibitions to talk with prospects about giving. Commonsense is not necessarily more common in times of economic challenge. Regardless of economic stress fueling personal stress, the leaders of organizations who discussed with board members and other lead donors what constituted good practice for fundraising in these times kept advancement efforts moving forward. Organizations with strong leadership generally fared best, along with others who still found ways to re-establish clarity and unity of purpose.

Advancement Engagement

In organizations that were facing serious financial stress before the downturn, unsurprisingly, these troubles were further magnified. Some too-often-heard differences of opinion among organizational leaders about the appropriate philosophy, roles, and processes for institutional advancement were amplified. Organizational leaders unable or unwilling to be responsive to the new financial landscape really needed to move rapidly from what David Weerts describes as the traditional model to an engagement model of advancement.[7]

Briefly, organizations following a traditional model for advancement focus effort toward matching the cultivation, solicitation, and stewardship of stakeholders by department affiliation or degree (in the case of alumni). For the engagement model, however, organizations articulate the overall vision and needs of the school/college/university in the context of the community agenda. As the name implies, the engagement model aligns stakeholders with their strongest current interests among the organization's initiatives to meet the community's needs, engaging stakeholders most closely with what matches their interests to advance the community's agenda[8]–paying no heed to the silos of the academy that are based on disciplines. If the traditional model assumes the educational institution to be the repository of knowledge, the engagement model assumes stakeholders from the community are participants with the educators in the development of knowledge, especially about ways to solve problems or address primary concerns of the community.

In a time of economic meltdown, the organizations best positioned to handle some of the realities of economic challenge were already functioning more in the engagement model, or were at least able to put together "collegial conversations" between internal and community leaders. These organizations tended to be flexible enough to respond to the changing stakeholder interests and capabilities in a dynamic economy.

The substantial economic changes of 1987, 1990-91, 2001, and 2008 all produced restructurings of capital, industries, and jobs. Leaders engaging stakeholders were sufficiently in touch with the economic changes to seek out and listen to pertinent community leaders to identify new linkage opportunities. These were the organizational leaders best able to sustain fundraising success.

For example, some large technology companies in times of economic challenge shed large numbers of jobs designed to develop services or products no longer needed in the changed economy—and therefore not needed for the next stage of the company's operations or technology development. Concurrently with announcing such job losses, these firms often increase recruiting for newly designed jobs, requiring different skill sets to support the company's next stages of development.

Although education and industry organizations operate on different time cycles for adjusting the design of programs, an advancement function based on the engagement model will obtain early-stage understandings of what is going on in the community. These insights enable "listening" educational leaders to align the academy to meet changes occurring in the community. Times of flux can provide an opportunity for education to adjust the operations and emphases of educational programs to match changing community needs.

Organizational Case Study

To illustrate characteristics of an engagement model of institutional advancement, along with providing a way to agree priorities for evolving this model, the following case study was designed for use in the workshop of chancellors, presidents, and other senior leaders of liberal arts colleges mentioned earlier.

Specifically, the challenge assigned to the workshop participants was to propose priority actions to sustain and expand fundraising for the next five years, in the lean economic conditions of 2009. The case study was used to help identify concerns that needed to be addressed for each of three distinct "Ages" of institutional advancement, namely "Formative", "Emergent," and "Mature." Generic descriptions of these different "Ages" of advancement evolution, as outlined later in this paper, were provided to workshop participants.

The hypothetical organization was named "College of Arts and Sciences Advancement" (or "CASA"), and the "facts" outlined were typical of a liberal arts college to provide a familiar framework for workshop participants. Three groups, with seven participants in each group, addressed one of the "Ages" of institutional advancement named.

Using the description of the pertinent "Age," each group was charged to suggest for CASA preferable approaches to:

- Reposition Strategy (Step 1)
- Organize Advancement Process (Step 2), and
- Integrate Priority Behaviors (Step 3)

Each group compiled a list of "TO DOs" for these steps, and then selected only the top priority for each step. The priorities recommended by the groups to grow funding in the tough economy, in each of the "Ages" of advancement, are noted later in this paper (Table 1).

Questions Each Group Considered

The questions distributed to guide each group's determination of priorities were:

Step 1: Reposition Strategy: How would you determine why your organization is uniquely valued? From whom would you seek input to describe the value of the organization and its programs? What would you most like to know from whom? Why? What is a good-sized board of trustees for advancement purposes?

Step 2: Organize Advancement Process: Which prospects (or suspects) should you engage most closely and ask? How do you determine what funds should be raised for, and how much should be requested of prospects? What tracking of outreach needs to be in place? How should the advancement budget be set? Why?

Step 3: Integrate Priority Behaviors: What are priority activities for each of the following: trustees, senior management, and advancement staff? Who are the key members of your advancement team? What is a good rate of visits to engage prospects and ask for major gifts? Who should you engage in advocacy, door-opening, asking, or follow-up? Why?

Facts about CASA

The facts describing the institutional advancement function at its three ages of evolution were:

CASA – Formative Age

Organization has some name recognition, though mainly in local and regional communities. Has a reputation for delivering programs well, including program-related events and occasions that foster interaction with the community.

Some trustees bring a variety of community leaders to the organization to meet the president and tour facilities or attend events. Most trustees regularly

91

attend meetings related to board activities and important public events. For more than a year, the advancement function has not been led most appropriately.

Fundraising targets are set based on the previous year's achievement, with annual adjustments that are influenced somewhat by expectations of trustees, program leaders, and/or other stakeholders. The list of potential larger donors is still being developed and these folks are yet to be systematically engaged. Philanthropic income is not yet four times the size of the advancement budget.

CASA – Emergent Age

Organization has good name recognition and reputation among most key stakeholders. Community outreach programs are many and the number of community members attending events in a variety of interest areas is continuously high.

A small percentage of trustees use personal networks to bring their contacts to events and follow through with the president and/or program leaders to find a match for giving. The president and an experienced leader of the advancement function cooperate to build outreach through trustees and vigorously drive advancement staff visits to some key stakeholder groups.

The comprehensive campaign target for the quiet phase of a campaign was set before the most recent economic downturn, with some years further to run on the original timeline for the campaign. Most of the identified larger prospects have been solicited. Philanthropic income is more than five times the size of the advancement budget.

CASA – Mature Age

Organization has national and international name recognition among key stakeholders. Program leaders and other staff are much sought after as expert commentators or participants for significant community undertakings, including public and corporate policy input. Seminars and cultural events of the organization are generally regarded as the reference in the field.

A substantial percentage of trustees and program advisory boards are well-networked philanthropists and corporate leaders, who have decision-making oversight of significant budgets themselves and who recommend and facilitate engagements of key philanthropists with the college. After ten years at this institution, the experienced leader of the advancement function is now working with her third president to strengthen further the number and quality of well-networked philanthropists, who will be recruited as trustees and advisory board members to help sustain the institution's leaders in key program areas.

The annual targets for philanthropy are determined by the president in consultation with advancement volunteers, deans of faculty, and advancement staff leadership. These are the people expected to collaborate to build fundraising teams of colleagues, community leaders and advancement staff to grow philanthropic income. Although the organization's most recent major campaign was successfully completed as the economic downturn was commencing, and philanthropic income has not declined overall, larger gifts are being secured from fewer donors and donor retention has declined. Philanthropic income annually is more than ten times the advancement budget.

Summary: Advancement Plan Priorities

After workshop participants identified and reviewed issues stimulated by the questions and facts outlined, they recommended the priority actions shown in Table 1.

	Formative	Emergent	Mature
Reposition strategy	Create centers of excellence.	Clarify the role of trustees to seek resonance with the community through outreach.	Use networks to find new donors.
Organize advancement process	Set advancement goals to address needs and establish a central advancement organization.	Initiate six-month review for how each part of advancement contributes to raising funds for the institution.	Add advancement staff, refresh the case for fund raising and identify the institution's program experts to be engaged in fundraising.
Integrate priority behaviors	President to set the agenda with priority on getting the President into the community.	Secure firm commitments from trustees to funding and fundraising.	President to commit serious time to fundraising.

Table 1: Advancement Plan Priorities: Case Study

Most evident in this summary of the groups' priorities for each "Age" of advancement was the similarity of emphasizing a pro-active responsibility of trustees and the president to engage the College leaders with the community. The priorities nicely summarize steps pertinent for an engagement model for advancement. With a little adjustment to take account of the maturity of an advancement effort, perhaps some combination of all that the workshop participants suggested above might be a valuable starter-kit to grow many advancement efforts, in either the best or worst economic conditions.

Best Practice?

Briefly, the priorities for advancement leaders to sustain fundraising success are focused efforts to:

1. **Reposition organizational strategy,** to engage stakeholders very closely, sharing why the organization is valued.
2. **Organize the advancement process** to focus priority actions within teams of the right trustees, leaders of academic or other key programs, and advancement professionals, partnered with the president–to set the pace for vigorous outreach to major gift prospects.
3. **Integrate priority behaviors** that make connecting conversations happen, to move forward big opportunities every day.

Leaders who advance such actions will reach out to the right prospects on the right big opportunities. Especially during times of economic stress, it will be the thoughtful and personal presentation of well-grounded dreams that is most likely to attract favor. This outreach might sometimes result in a relatively small number of successful solicitations in an economic downturn, but personal engagement in difficult times will often be especially welcomed. Such efforts potentially have great impact over time, where relationships are sustained.

Putting together the recommendations from the leadership workshop with my ongoing surveys of how institutional advancement leaders responded to the tough times, the following is a composite of best practices suggested for sustaining fundraising success:

1. State what gifts are now especially meaningful.
2. Engage trustees, foundations, and individuals with large capacity for giving, whose interests are closely matched with the gift opportunities.
3. Emphasize systematic efforts to identify new prospects for larger gifts.
4. Revisit and solicit past donors of larger gifts.
5. Seek endowment and other gifts that will assure longer-term financial security for the organization, including pledges over multiple years and planned gifts.
6. Speak to the specific impacts of a gift and be ready, especially during the solicitation of a larger gift, for the donor to want to be spread payments over several years.
7. Build a very close-knit team, consisting of the president, chief financial officer, and the leader of advancement, with regular open discussion and joint problem-solving.
8. Increase the prospect pool and the number of "love" visits and calls to prospects and donors.
9. Redouble all personal contact, especially solicitation.

Building Advancement Performance

The turbulence of economic flux clearly increases the need to be aligned in strategy, processes, and behaviors. Times of economic challenge provide rather too many opportunities for confusion of views about the most productive actions for an organization's advancement, with old anxieties and mythologies about fundraising potentially popping up in unexpected ways.

One way to agree expectations and understandings is through purposeful, open conversations to develop a soundly based, written plan of action that takes account of the concerns of board members, the chief executive, and the leader of institutional advancement. Some consultative process of this type can help to address concerns that might otherwise become distractions or excuses for inaction. During the extended efforts needed to build long-term successes in fundraising, it is best to remember the wisdom that, just as for the overall reputation of an organization, it takes both time and focused effort to build the successes that shape reputations in institutional advancement.

Comparative Growth

For perspective on what constitutes fundraising accomplishment in different universities over time, the following metrics (Table 2) were derived in a benchmarking project.[9] These points of comparison were collected via advancement leaders from four countries, in five organizations that commenced fundraising at different times during five decades.

	USA 1	USA 2	Canada	UK	Australia
First Year of Fund Raising	1936	1960	1946	1990	1987
Fund Raising Income/year	$182M	$27M	$37M	$1.3M	$1.5M
Endowment	$2.7B	$262M	-	$8M	$184,000
Number of Fund Raising Field Staff	85	18	16	11	4
Alumni of Record	129,160	57,449	120,000	45,000	1,600
Major Gift Officer Visits/month	15	27	12	14	12
Major Gift Officer Asks/month	4	4	3	2	2

Table 2: Higher Education Reality Check

The table identifies the age of advancement operations, scale of fundraising income, size of endowment, number of "field" fundraising professionals, number of alumni of record, estimated average number of visits of a major gift officer each month, and an estimated average number of "asks" or solicitations managed by a major gift officer each month.

The facts recorded in Table 2 can provide a reality check on unfettered conversations about the growth targets and processes appropriate for a particular organization. It is important for the organizational leader, board members, advancement, and academic or program leaders to base decisions about goals for fundraising on mutually understood realities before setting out together to raise funds. This decision-making about goals requires careful assessment of the maturity of the advancement function, the level of engagement and philanthropic capability of an organization's constituency groups, the extent of existing engagement with well-networked philanthropists, and the extent to which organizational leaders truly "walk the talk" in fundraising.

The differences of what might be accomplished by "Formative," "Emergent," or "Mature" advancement efforts are particularly important to keep in mind. Although it is difficult to generalize about what constitutes a mature advancement function, because of variations in constituencies, the age of a program, and many other factors, some guide to what characterizes a mature advancement function might include:

- Cost/Revenue at less than 20 percent, with some organizations that are conducting a comprehensive campaign or have a strong major gifts program sometimes able to accomplish costs of less than 6 percent.
- Annual fund at 10 percent of total giving.
- Solicitation of bequests coordinated by each planned giving officer at a rate or 1-2 per month.
- 40-50 "hot prospects" managed at any time by each major gift officer.
- Major gift officer (after three years) expected to manage 150-200 prospects, with potentially $600,000 to $3M plus per year in gifts, depending on the characteristics of the constituency and other factors.
- Up to 6-8 involvements to ask a prospect for a major gift.

New Practices in Tough Times

New economic challenges bring both opportunities and new requirements for organizational leaders to develop new flexibilities to advance effective engagement of prospective donors. Some emphases within the actions that strengthen institutional advancement efforts will differ from one organization to another, according to the "Age" of institutional advancement efforts, styles of leadership, and organizational priorities. But a constant is to ensure attention to priorities concerned with (1) strategy, (2) process, and (3) behavior.[10] To grow funding in tough times, careful consideration of ways to develop best practice in all three of these areas is required.

Leaders who embrace considered efforts to **R**eposition strategy, **O**rganize advancement processes, and **I**ntegrate priority behaviors will be well equipped

96

to maximize an organization's **R**eturn **O**n **I**nvestment for the advancement function. In the worst or best of economic times, delivering this return on investment by successfully growing external funding requires ever closer cooperation, coordination, and communication among the advancement team, consisting of the CEO, governing board, and leader of institutional advancement.

NOTE: This paper collects thoughts shared for a workshop of chancellors, presidents, and other senior leaders of state liberal arts colleges titled "Sustain Funding Growth: Leadership Guide to Navigate Tough Times," at the 2009 Conference of the Council of Public Liberal Arts Colleges, Keene State College, Keene, NH

References

1. Brown, J. (2009), "University of Oregon Raises Record $853 million in Campaign Oregon," January 30, *Pmr.uoregon.edu*
2. Gerritsen, J. (2008), "New Zealand: University's $100M Fundraising Campaign," *Universityworldnews.com*
3. _____ (2009), "Indiana University Foundation–IU Raises Matching the Promise Goal to $1.1B," *IUfoundation.iu.edu*
4. _____ (2009), "Over Half of Companies Increase Their Philanthropy in 2008, Despite Economic Decline," June 2, *Corporatephilanthropy.org*
5. Blackbaud, Inc. (2009), Target Analytics Index of Higher Education Fundraising Performance Q4 2008, April 14, *Blackbaud.com*
6. Miller, Rodney G. (2009), *Pooled Research Study: Best Practices in Tough Economic Times*, TS, Author's private collection
7. Weerts, D.J. (2007), "Toward an Engagement Model of Institutional Advancement at Public Colleges and Universities," *International Journal of Educational Advancement*, 7(2), pp. 96-7
8. Weerts, p. 97
9. Miller, Rodney G. (1994), *Benchmarking for Major Gift Growth: Project Description*, Brisbane, Qld: Queensland University of Technology
10. Miller, Rodney G. (1995), "Briefing to Benchmark Institutional Advancement," *AITEA Conference*, Gold Coast, Qld

Bibliography

_____ (2009), "Indiana University Foundation–IU Raises Matching the Promise Goal to $1.1B," *IUfoundation.iu.edu*

_____ (2009), "Over Half of Companies Increase Their Philanthropy in 2008, Despite Economic Decline," June 2, *Corporatephilanthropy.org*

Allert, J.R. and S.R. Chatterjee (1997), "Corporate Communication and Trust in Leadership," *Corporate Communications: An International Journal*, 2(1), pp. 14-21

Andersen, M.A. (2010), "Creating *esprit de corps* in Times of Crisis: Employee Identification with Values in a Danish Windmill Company," *Corporate Communications: An International Journal*, 15(1), pp. 102-23

Appelbaum, S.H., R. Lopes, L. Audet, A. Steed, M. Jacob, T. Augustinas, and D. Manolopoulos (2003), "Communication during Downsizing of a Telecommunications Company," *Corporate Communications: An International Journal*, 8(2), pp. 73-96

Batten, J. D. (1989), *Tough-Minded Leadership*, New York: American Management Association

Bay, Christian (1977), "Human Needs and Political Education," in Fitzgerald, R. (Ed.), *Human Needs and Politics*, Sydney: Pergamon

Bennis, Warren G. (1989), *On Becoming a Leader*, Reading, Mass.: Addison-Wesley

Bennis, Warren G and B. Nanus (1985), *Leaders: The Strategies for Taking Charge*, New York: Harper and Row

Bishop, B. (2006), "Theory and Practice Converge: a Proposed Set of Corporate Communication Principles," *Corporate Communications: An International Journal*, 11(3), pp. 214-31

Blackbaud, Inc. (2009), Target Analytics Index of Higher Education Fundraising Performance Q4 2008, April 14, *Blackbaud.com*

Bolton, R., R.E. Freeman, J. Harris, B. Moriarity, L. Nash, M. Wing (2009), *The Dynamics of Public Trust in Business–Emerging Opportunities for Leaders: A Call to Action to Overcome the Present Crisis of Trust in Business*, New York: Arthur W. Page Society and Business Roundtable Institute for Corporate Ethics

Bostock, William W. (1975), "The Linguistic and Cultural Bases for Australian Democracy," *Plural Societies*, [The Hague], Winter, 6(4)

Brown, J. (2009), "University of Oregon Raises Record $853 million in Campaign Oregon," January 30, *Pmr.uoregon.edu*

Brown, J.A.C. (1963), *Techniques of Persuasion: From Propaganda to Brainwashing*, Harmondsworth: Pelican

Burnet, Ken (1993), "Relationship Fund Raising," Conference of the Fundraising Institute of Australia, Brisbane, Qld

Carbone, Robert F. (1989), *Fundraising as a Profession*, College Park, MD: Clearinghouse for Research on Fundraising, University of Maryland

Carleton, W.G. (1951), "Effective Speech in a Democracy," *Southern Speech Journal*, 17, pp. 2-13

Chaffee, S.H. (1975), *Political Communication: Issues and Strategies for Research*, Thousand Oaks, CA: Sage

Chodkjewicz, Andrezej (1978) Interview with researcher, October 11

Chodkjewicz, Andrezej (1978), *Political Communication: Turkish Community in Sydney*, TS, Author's private collection

Clarke, G. and L.W. Murray (2000), "Investor Relations: Perceptions of the Annual Statement," *Corporate Communications: An International Journal*, 5(3), pp. 144-51

Clarke, Marcus (1877), "A Tall, Coarse, Strong-jawed, Greedy, Pushing, Talented Man," quoted in Turner, Ian (Ed.), *The Australian Dream*, Melbourne: Sun, pp. 132-3

Clevenger, T. (1960), "Speaker and Society: The Role of Freedom in a Democratic State," *Southern Speech Journal*, 26, pp. 93-9

Courts, D.C. Head, English, Churchlands CAE, communication with author

Crocker, W.J. (1977), "Teaching Oracy in the English Programme," *English in Australia*, February, 39, pp. 54-8

Crocker, W.J. (1979), "Approaches to the Teaching of Oral Communication," Conference on Developing Oral Communication Competence, University of New England and Armidale College of Advanced Education, Armidale NSW, Australia, July

Cushman, Donald P. (1995), "Continuous Improvement and International Benchmarking," Conference on Benchmarking High Performance Organizations, Oahu, Hawaii

Cushman, Donald P. and Sarah S. King (1993), "Visions of Order: High-Speed Management in the Private Sector of the Global Marketplace," in Kozminski, A.K. and Donald P. Cushman, *Organizational Communication and Management: A Global Perspective*, Albany, NY: State University of New York Press, pp. 69-83

Cushman, Donald P. and Sarah S. King (1994), "The Nature, Function, and Scope of High-Speed Management Leadership," Inter-University Center Conference on Organizational Communication, Sydney, Australia

Dean, R.L. (1955), "Aspects of Persuasive Appeal in Stevenson's Campaign Speeches," *The Speaker*, May

Dixon, T.C. (1990), "Reorganizing a University," *Australian Journal of Communication*, 17(3), pp. 38-63

Doyle, M. and W.A. Kraus (1982), *Senior Management Briefing: Improving Quality, Productivity, Harmony and Profitability*, Author's private collection

Drucker, Peter F. (1990), *Managing the Non-Profit Organization: Practices and Principles*, Oxford: Butterworth-Heinemann

Duck, J.D. (1993), "Managing Change: The Art of Balancing," *Harvard Business Review,* November-December, pp. 109-18

Ellul, Jacques (1965), *Propaganda: The Formation of Men's Attitudes,* New York: Vintage

Ellul, Jacques (1973), *The New Demons,* New York: Seabury

Elving, W.J.L. (2010), "Trends and Developments within Corporate Communication: An Analysis of Ten Years of *CCIJ*", *Corporate Communications: An International Journal,* 15(1), pp. 5-8

Elving, W.J.L. (2005), "The Role of Communication in Organisational Change", *Corporate Communications: An International Journal,* 10(2), pp. 129-38

Edelman (2009), *2009 Edelman Trust Barometer,* New York: Edelman

Edelman (2010), *2010 Edelman Trust Barometer,* New York: Edelman

Fagen, R. (1966), *Politics and Communication,* Boston: Little Brown

Freedman, J. (2009), *The Motivation Iceberg,* Freedom, CA: 6-Seconds

Freedman, J. (2010), *Change Failure: April 6 Web-Workshop,* Freedom, CA: 6-Seconds

Galetzka, M., D. Gelders, J.P. Verckens, and E. Seydel (2008), "Transparency and Performance Communication: a Case Study of Dutch Railways," *Corporate Communications: An International Journal,* 13(4), pp. 433-47

Genest, C.M. (2005), "Cultures, Organizations and Philanthropy," *Corporate Communications: An International Journal,* 10(4), pp. 315-27

Gerritsen, J. (2008), "New Zealand: University's $100M Fundraising Campaign," *Universityworldnews.com*

Goodman, M.B. (2005), "Restoring Trust in American Business: The Struggle to Change Perception," *Journal of Business Strategy,* 26(4), pp. 29-37

Goodman, M.B. (1995), "Organizational Inertia or Corporate Culture Momentum," in Cushman, D.P. and S.S. King (Eds.), *Communicating Organizational Change: A Management Perspective,* State University of New York Press, Albany NY, pp. 95-112

Grey, A. (n.d.), "Who is Literate?" *Literacy Discussion,* 7(2), pp. 37-55

Groombridge, Brian (1972), *Television and the People: A Programme for Democratic Participation,* Harmondsworth: Penguin

Halloran, S.M. (1975), "On the End of Rhetoric: Classical and Modern," *College English,* February, 36(6), pp. 621-31

Horovitz, B. (2002), "Trust", *USA Today,* July 16, p. 1

Hymes, D. (1975), "On Communication Competence," excerpts in Pride, J.B. and J. Holmes (Eds.), *Sociolinguistics: Selected Readings,* Harmondsworth: Penguin, p. 269-93

Ingram, D.E. (1976), "Something There Is That Doesn't Love a Wall: Current Developments in Foreign Language Teaching," *Audio Visual Language Journal,* 14(2), pp. 71-85

Ingram, D.E. (1978), "Education for Pluralism: The Changing Role of Language Teaching in Australia," in Ingram, D.E. and T.J. Quinn (Eds.), *Language Learning in Australia,* Melbourne: Australian International

Jones, J.W. (1993), *High-Speed Management: Time-Based Strategies for Managers and Organizations,* San Francisco: Jossey-Bass

Jorgensen, P.E., M. Isaksson (2008), "Building Credibility in International Banking and Financial Markets: A Study of How Corporate Reputations Are Managed through

Image Advertising", *Corporate Communications: An International Journal,* 13(4), pp. 365-79

Johannesen, R.L. (2010), "Perspectives on Ethics in Persuasion", in Larson, C.U., *Persuasion: Reception and Responsibility,* Boston, MA: Wadsworth, pp. 41-69

Kellen, Konrad (1965), "Introduction" to Jacques Ellul's *Propaganda: The Formation of Men's Attitudes,* New York: Vintage, p. v-viii

Kelley, S. (1960), *Political Campaigning: Problems in Creating an Informed Electorate,* Washington DC: Brookings Institution

Kiechel, W. (1993), "How We Will Work in the Year 2000," *Fortune,* May 17, pp. 30-7

Lerner, D. (1972), "Effective Propaganda," in Lerner, D. (Ed.), *Propaganda in War and Crisis,* New York: Arno

Levin, Murray B. (1962), "Political Strategy for the Alienated Voter," *Public Opinion Quarterly,* 26, pp. 47-63

Lippmann, Lorna (1976), "Literacy and Ethnic Minorities in Australia," *Literacy Discussion,* Summer, 7(2), pp. 23-35

Lippmann, Walter (1960), "The Indispensable Opposition," in Eastman, A.M., and others (Eds.), *The Norton Reader,* New York: Norton, pp. 1006-12

Lucero, M., A.T.T Kwang, and A. Pang (2009), "Crisis Leadership: When Should the CEO Step Up?" *Corporate Communications: An International Journal,* 14(3), pp. 234-48

McLellan, David (1978), "Political Theory," in Inglis, Fred *Literature and Environment,* quoted in Crick, Bernard and Alex Porter (Eds.), *Political Education and Political Literacy,* London: Longman

McGoldrick, W.P. and K.E. Osborne (1993), *An Audit of the Advancement Program: Queensland University of Technology,* TS, Author's private collection

McKinnon, K.R. (Chairman) (1978), *Report for the Triennium 1979-81,* Canberra: Schools Commission

McKinnon, C. and Roslyn Petelin (2010), "Complying with Plain Language Guidelines in the Corporation: If Not, Why Not?" Conference of Corporate Communication International, CUNY at Wroxton College, Wroxton, UK

Meaney, J.W. (1951), "Propaganda as Psychical Coercion," *Review of Politics,* 13, pp. 64-87

Menzies, Robert G. (1955), *Address to the National Press Club,* Washington DC, March 16

Miller, C.R. (2004), "Expertise and Agency: Transformations of Ethos in Human-computer Interaction," in *The Ethos of Rhetoric,* Hyde, M.J. (Ed.), Columbia: University of South Carolina Press, pp. 197-218

Miller, Rodney G. [publications listed at conclusion of bibliography]

Magee, D. (2007), *How Toyota Became #1: Leadership Lessons from the World's Greatest Car Company,* New York: Portfolio

Olea, V.F. (n.d.), *Culture and Communication,* International Commission for the Study of Communication Problems, Document No. 75, Paris: UNESCO

Orwell, George (1954), 'Principles of Newspeak', *Nineteen Eighty-Four,* Harmondsworth: Penguin, pp. 241-51 [1st published 1949]

Orwell, George (1981), 'Politics and the English Language', *A Collection of Essays,* Orlando, FL: Harvest, pp. 156-71 [1st published 1946]

Phillips, D. (2006), "Relationships Are the Core Value for Organizations: A Practitioner Perspective," *Corporate Communications: An International Journal*, 11(1), pp. 34-42.

Port, O., J. Cary, K. Kelley, and S. Forest (1992), "Quality," *Business Week*, November 30, pp. 66-72

The PR Coalition. (2003), *Restoring Trust in Business: Models for Action*, New York: Arthur W. Page Society

Raine, K. (1970), *William Blake*, London: Thames and Hudson

Rosso, Henry A. (1989), "Principles and Techniques of Effective Fund Raising– Fundamentals Course," Oakland, CA: The Fund Raising School, January

Rosso, Henry A. (1991), *Achieving Excellence in Fund Raising: A Comprehensive Guide to Principles, Strategies, and Methods*, San Francisco: Jossey-Bass

Saint-Gaudens, A., (2009), *Augustus Saint-Gaudens: Master of American Sculpture*. December 28 Television Broadcast on KTEH

Salem, P. (2008), "The Seven Communication Reasons Organizations Do Not Change," *Corporate Communications: An International Journal*, 13(3), pp. 333-48.

Scanlan, Ross (1961), "The Nazi Rhetorician," in Howes, Raymond F. (Ed.), *Historical Studies of Rhetoric and Rhetoricians*, Ithaca: Cornell University Press, pp. 352-65

Seglin, J.L. (2002), "Restoring Trust in Corporate America", *Time*, July 9

Shannon, C. E., W. Weaver (1949), *The Mathematical Theory of Communication*, Urbana, IL: University of Illinois Press

Sheldon, K. (1996), "Credibility is Risky Business: An Interview with Vincent T. Covell," *Communication World*, April, pp. 16-9

6 Seconds. (2009), *Organizational Vital Signs*, Freedom, CA: 6 Seconds

Shockley-Zalabak, P., Morreale, S., and Hackman, M.Z. (2010), *Building the High-Trust Organization: Strategies for Supporting Five Key Dimensions of Trust*, San Francisco: Jossey-Bass

Smythe, J. (1997) "The Changing Role of Internal Communication in Tomorrow's Company," *Corporate Communications: An International Journal*, 2(1), pp. 4-7

Stenhouse, Lawrence (1967), *Culture and Education*, London: Nelson, quoted in Ipswich State High School English Curriculum Guide, Ipswich, Australia

Stewart, T. (1994), "How to Lead a Revolution," *Fortune*, November 28, pp. 22-33

Strong, James (1993), "Chief Executive Comment," *The Australian Way*, December, p. 4

Thayer, Lee (2007), *How Executives Fail: 25 Surefire Recipes for Sabotaging Your Career*, Rochester, NY: Windsor

Thayer, Lee (n.d.), *Making High-Performance Organizations: The Logic of Virtuosity*, TS, Author's private collection

Tully, S. (1993), "The Real Key to Creating Wealth," *Fortune*, September 20, pp. 34-42

Tuominen, P. (1997), "Investor Relations: A Nordic School Approach," *Corporate Communications: An International Journal*, 2(1), pp. 46-55

Watson, T., S. Osborne-Brown, and M. Longhurst (2002), "Issues Negotiation™ – Investing in Stakeholders," *Corporate Communications: An International Journal*, 7(1), pp. 54-61

Wanguri, D.M. (2003), "Federally Regulated Corporate Communication: An Analysis of Dominant Values," *Corporate Communications: An International Journal*, 8(3), pp. 163-72

Wells, D. (1979), *The Deep North*, Collingwood, Vic: Outback

Weerts, D.J. (2007), "Toward an Engagement Model of Institutional Advancement at Public Colleges and Universities," *International Journal of Educational Advancement*, 7(2), pp. 79-103

Whitlam, E. Gough (1975), *Address to the National Press Club*, Washington DC, 8 May

Wilkinson, A. (1971), *Foundations of Language: Talking and Reading in Young Children*, London: Oxford University Press

Williams, Raymond (1976), *Keywords: A Vocabulary of Culture and Society*, London: Fontana

Worth, Michael J. and James W. Asp III (1994), *The Development Officer in Higher Education: Toward an Understanding of the Role*, Washington DC: George Washington University, Clearinghouse on Higher Education

Representative Publications - The following is a selection of my publications, including conference and webinar presentations.

1976-1987 (Editor) *Australian Journal of Communication* (initially published as *Australian SCAN)*, Brisbane, Qld: The Communication Institute

1976a "Polemic and Propaganda in Australian Election Campaigns," *Conference on Interpersonal and Mass Communication, held at The New South Wales Institute of Technology, Sydney, 8th to 10th December [1976]: Conference Proceedings*, Kensington, NSW: Clarendon Press, pp. 195-212

1976b "Image Making and Australian Political Rhetoric," *Inter Connections*, 1(1), pp. 20-5

1976c "Speech Preparation for the Professional Person," *Australian Scan*, 1(1), pp. 1-7

1977 "The Quiet Rhetoric of Sir Samuel Walker Griffith," *Australian Scan: Journal of Human Communication*, 3, pp. 59-65

1979a "After the Evolution? Language for Social Comment in Germaine Greer's Book, *The Female Eunuch*," Conference of the Applied Linguistics Association of Australia, Sydney, NSW: The University of Sydney

1979b "The Role of the Speech in Presenting Your Company," *Rydges*, 52(11), pp. 103-4

1980a "Developing Oral Communication in a Pluralistic Society: Rhetors and the Democratic Process," in Crocker, W.J. (Ed.), *Developing Oral Communication Competence*, Armidale, NSW, The University of New England, pp. 85-91

1980b "Freedom of Information by 2000 A.D.?: Gaining Access to the Meaning of Government Communication," in *Science for a Sustainable Society: Communication*, Proceedings of the Jubilee Congress of the Australian and New Zealand Association for the Advancement of Science, The University of Adelaide, Adelaide, SA, pp. 318-26

1980c "Finding Communication Meaning in Australia," Inaugural Organizing Conference of Australian Communication Association, College of Arts and Education, Raywood, SA

1981 "Rhetoric of democracy: Communication and the Politics of Information," in Ward, W.T. and M.M. Bryden (Eds.), *Public Information: Your Right to Know*, Brisbane, Qld: Royal Society of Queensland, pp. 15-20

1982 "The Measure of Menzies's Public Language Style," 52nd Congress of the Australian and New Zealand Association for the Advancement of Science, Macquarie University, Sydney, NSW

1983a "Language Styles for Public Communication: Research into Practice," in Smith, T.J. (Ed.), *Communication in Australia*, Proceedings of Conference of Australian Communication Association held at Kuring-gai College of Advanced Education, Warrnambool, Vic: Warrnambool Institute Press, pp. 123-8

1983b "Planning Communication with Cost-benefit Analysis and Issues Management," International Conference on Organisational Communication, Warrnambool Institute of Advanced Education, Melbourne, Vic

1984a "Winning the TV Election," *Australian Journalism Review*, 6(2), July-December, pp. 36-9

1984b "Leaders Debate Deserves Attention," *Communicator*, 1(2), p. 1

1985a "Dimensions of Communicative Competence in the 1983 Federal Election Campaign: Fraser v. Hawke," in Osborne, G., R. Penman, D. Sless (Eds.), *Communication in Government*, Proceedings of Conference on Communication and Government, Canberra College of Advanced Education, Canberra, ACT, pp. 113-9

1985b "Beyond Word-processing: Computer Assistance for the Professional Writer," *Australian Journalism Review*, 7(1&2), January-December, pp. 116-7

1985c, with Roslyn Petelin, "This and Now: Policy and Process for Developing Literacy," 4th National Australian Reading Association Conference, July, Brisbane, Qld

1986 "Relationship in Language: A Framework for Computer Analysis of Language," Conference of Australian Communication Association, Australian National University, Canberra, ACT

1987 "Leadership through Communication–In Developing High Performance Organisations," *Australian Journal of Communication*, 12, pp. 1-8.

1990 "Fundraising Results through Corporate Communication," *Australian Journal of Communication*, 17(1), pp. 74-80

1994 *Benchmarking for Major Gift Growth: Project Description*, Brisbane, Qld: Queensland University of Technology

1995 "Improving Community Service: Strategic Cooperation through Communication," in Cushman, Donald P. and Sarah Sanderson King (Eds.), *Communicating Organizational Change: A Management Perspective*, Albany, NY: State University of New York Press, pp. 65-81

2001 "Beyond Benchmarking Institutional Advancement: Jump-start to Fund-raising Excellence," in Cushman, Donald P. and Sarah Sanderson King (Eds.), *Excellence in Communicating Organizational Strategy*, Albany, NY: State University of New York Press, pp. 139-62

2009a "Sustain Funding Growth: Leadership Guide to Navigate Tough Times," Conference of the Council of Public Liberal Arts Colleges, Keene State College, Keene, NH

2009b *Pooled Research Study: Best Practices in Tough Economic Times*, TS, Author's private collection

2010a "Developing the Culture of Trust in which Large-Scale Gains Become Possible," Conference of Corporate Communication International, CUNY at Wroxton College, Wroxton, UK

2010b *Major Gift Strategies that Work,* June 30, Nonprofit Webinars, Slideshare

2011a *Leaders' Communication Strategies for Large-Scale Gains,* Conference of Corporate Communication International, Baruch College-CUNY, New York, NY

2011b *Advancement Best Practices that Work,* August 10, Nonprofit Webinars, Slideshare

2011c *Why, When and How the Big Gift Campaigns Work,* March 16, Nonprofit Webinars, Slideshare

2012a *Best Practices to Advance Planned Giving,* October 19, Nonprofit Webinars, Slideshare

2012b *Big Giving Results,* September 19, Nonprofit Webinars, Slideshare

2013 *Transformational Advancement,* June 19, Nonprofit Webinars, Slideshare

2022a *Australians Speak Out: Persuasive Language Styles,* Albany, NY: Parula Press

2022b *Communication & Beyond,* Albany, NY: Parula Press

Acknowledgments

My thanks go to many colleagues and students, and to the leaders of universities or corporate, government, and community organizations across five nations for the opportunity to explore thoughts distilled in these essays. I am grateful to many people at different levels within high-performance organizations.

With special appreciation to the institutional advancement leaders, who so willingly offered insights and experiences that inform the essays, at Amherst College, Harvard University, Indiana University–Purdue University at Indianapolis, King's College University of London, London Business School, McGill University, Manchester University, Massachusetts Institute of Technology, Merton College (Oxford), Oxford University-Central Campaign, Queensland University of Technology, Rensselaer Polytechnic Institute, St Catherine's College (Oxford), Stanford University, and University of Strathclyde.

Also appreciated are the opportunities afforded to share thoughts in papers presented at The Royal Society of Queensland, Corporate Communication International, and The Council for Advancement and Support of Education, as well as with universities and industry organizations internationally.

Grateful acknowledgment is made to the State University of New York Press, for permission to reprint the essays in chapters four and six. These were first published respectively in 1995 as "Improving community service: Strategic cooperation through communication," in *Communicating Organizational Change: A Management Perspective*, pp. 65-81 and in 2001 as "Beyond benchmarking institutional advancement: Jump-start to fund-raising excellence," in *Excellence in Communicating Organizational Strategy*, pp. 139-62.

As always, I acknowledge with many thanks my wife, family, and friends, whose support, candor, and patience are always generously given.

About the Author

Rodney G. Miller writes about communication. He is published by the State University of New York Press, other universities, and The Royal Society of Queensland, with early writing published in *The Australian* newspaper.

His book, *Australians Speak Out: Persuasive Language Styles,* illustrates the persuasive strength of leaders who use ordinary words in extraordinary ways to make democracy thrive. It is the first detailed assessment of the public communication of these notable leaders from the 1890s to modern times. *Communication & Beyond* chronicles some people, principles, and practices responsible for a new dawning of communication education in Australia, offering new careers locally and internationally.

While teaching communication at Queensland University of Technology (QUT), he founded and edited *Australian Journal of Communication* for over a decade. He has since led external relations and the advancement of innovative education at QUT and universities in the United States and internationally, also consulting on communication, serving as adjunct faculty in fundraising at the Indiana University-Purdue University center on philanthropy, and chairing or serving on the governing boards of educational, professional, and community organizations.

Website: communicator.rodney-miller.com

www.ingramcontent.com/pod-product-compliance
Lightning Source LLC
Chambersburg PA
CBHW020751300326
41914CB00050B/70